HOPE *journey*

ROBERT HARTLEY AND AMYANN HARTLEY

Kansas City, Missouri

www.bobhartley.org

HOPE *journey*

By Robert Hartley and Amyann Hartley.
www.bobhartley.org

Copyright © 2010 by Deeper Waters, Inc.
Printed in the United States of America

ISBN: 978-0-615-36602-9

Cover/Interior Design: Chérie Blair
www.uniquedove.com

Editor: Michelle Van Loon
www.theparablelife.com

'Dear Hope Seekers, I have known Bob Hartley for at least twenty years, and God has always majorly had His hand on Bob's life. Now He is using Bob to teach us through his Ministry of Hope. Faith is the substance of things hoped for and evidence of things not seen. Knowing that the world today is in a crisis, afraid and lost; hope and trust is what we all need as God is changing the world. May the Lord bless this Ministry of Hope through this book."

In His Name, Rev. Rosey Grier
Author, Actor, Minister and NFL Legend

"Bob Hartley is one of the most respected and accurate prophetic voices of our times. His new book 'Hope Journey' is so exciting because hope is the most neglected of the big three Faith, Hope and Love. Hope is that something that we all can possess that begins our journey into faith's adventures! My wife Lori and I love Bob and are crazy about hope!"

Jim Bakker
Author, TV Personality (the Jim Bakker Show seen on Direct TV, Dish Network, Sky Angel, TCT network, CTN Network, World Harvest network and 9 live satellites around the world)

"Much has been written about Faith, and also Love yet seldom do we hear a message on Hope. Bob Hartley shares a life changing word on Hope, that is desperately needed in the complicated turmoil of today's world. This book will lift you up and keep you there."

John Arnott
International Speaker, Founding Pastor of the Toronto Airport Christian Fellowship, President of Catch the Fire Ministries and Overseer of Partners in Harvest Network of Churches.

"God has given Bob a powerful hope message that is changing the hearts of individuals, families, communities, cities and nations for the Kingdom."

Mitch Wheeler
Senior Director of Corporate Partnership Sales at Kansas City Royals

"In the 20 plus years that I have known Bob, I have yet to come across anyone who approaches his or her faith with as much conviction, vigor and devotion. Bob has a servant's heart like few I have ever seen and I am truly blessed to call him a friend, a mentor and most importantly, an example of someone who has started and will finish the race."

Grant Curtis
Film Producer of Spiderman 3, Co-Producer of Spiderman 1 & 2

"This is a great book, and a timely one. From a deep personal journey with God, full of great trials and many victories flows a rich understanding of the God of hope. This book will help the readers to beat despair and give power to build God's Kingdom on earth."

Dr. John C. Kim
Founder and President of JAMA (Jesus Awakening Movement in America/All Nations)

This book is dedicated to:

℘

OUR GOD,
WHO IS EVERLASTING HOPE.

MY WIFE,
WHO IS MY HOPE HERO.

MY CHILDREN,
WHO KEEP HOPE AND JOY
ALIVE EACH DAY.

MY FATHER AND MOTHER,
WHOSE LIVES HAVE
BEEN AN EVER-UNFOLDING
EXPRESSION OF HOPE.

AND

TO THE HOPE TEAM
IN KANSAS CITY
AND OUR FRIENDS ACROSS
THE WORLD THAT HAVE
COMMITTED TO BRING
A HOPE REFORMATION
TO CITIES AND NATIONS.

Table Of Contents

SECTION THREE: AN INVITATION TO GO
ON THE JOURNEY OF HOPE

FOREWORD

It's not often that I meet someone who has a life, message and family filled with as much hope as Bob Hartley. He's a refreshing carrier of the joy and hopefulness of heaven. Bob is an amazing God-send to me personally and to our Bethel family.

Hope Journey is a timely book for our world. The storm clouds of mistrust, disappointment and confusion have blanketed our society and could easily cause men's hearts to faint with hopelessness. It requires constant attention to not get swept along in the tumult of these persistent storm clouds. Yet, throughout history, there have always been rare men and women who have caught a vision above the clouds of doubt and despair... a vision filled with faith and hope for a reality and future that can't be seen with natural earth-bound eyes. They have learned to see more with their eyes closed than with their eyes open. And even though their circumstances may be meager, they know they have the "best view in town". That kind of vision can only be gotten from the God who delights to "call forth those things which are not, as though they were". He has seen our beginning and end, and has never lost hope for us.

All of Heaven is eagerly waiting for men and women who will pay the price to discover the heart of God and will dare to herald a message of hope in the face of the oppositional winds of popular opinion. If heeded, that herald will dispel the clouds of hopelessness and bring a much-needed revelation of hope. These epic occasions have eternally altered history as a mere human speaks anointed words of hope and life into mankind's fallen world. God's will is done on earth as we partner with His promises and vision, and speak them forth.

Here are some examples of the way a voice of hope has changed the course of history:

- David's slaying of Goliath - which created instant confidence and zeal in the armies of Israel

- Haggai's simple prophecy - "God is with you" - transforming all with "a mind to work"

- Nehemiah's stand on the wall - inspiring all to rebuild the walls of Jerusalem

- George Washington's visionary leadership to cross the Potomac led to a decisive victory over the Tories

- Martin Luther King's - "I have a dream", which still echoes, inspires and liberates today

- Joan of Arc's calming divine guidance led her fellow Frenchmen against oppression

- Winston Churchill's statesmanly voice of authority inspired England when it seemed about to fall to Nazism

In our day, a whole generation of hope reformers is emerging on the earth, both men and women who know that they can change their world with a powerful voice of hope. They are seated with Christ, they have the mind of Christ and have heard the secrets of heaven... and from that lofty position they confidently prophesy, "Let Your Kingdom come in the earth below even as it is here in the Heavens"! All of creation has been expectantly waiting for the emergence of these sons of God who see as God sees... and will speak with His authority, as the oracle of God.

Heaven longs to burst in upon this fallen world with a radical and transformational message of hope. In Hope Journey you'll find yourself awakened with God's desire to bring a hope-filled heaven to a hope-starved world.

In addition to Bob's message of hope, he has been graced with a public prophetic gift of unusual proportions. The clarity and poignancy of his gift has profoundly impacted me and has spoken directly into inner-level issues of Bethel Church. His prophetic gift has confirmed our path with uncanny timing and relevance... even reaching back into our past to validate a key word for the future. We've been profoundly reminded that our Lord truly knows every detail of our lives. It's truly refreshing and empowering to hear God speak with this level of detail and clarity. Bob's ministry style is decidedly personal and heartfelt... so heartfelt that it's easy to feel the friendship of God through his ministry. We have become, I believe, life-long friends.

A Godly man's message is strongly validated by his life and family. Bob, his wife Terry and their family are each spiritually alive with clear eyes for the future and a strong voice of hope. Bob's vibrant family is a crown to his message.

It is my joy to commend Bob Hartley's Hope Journey to you. His apropos insights are well presented and his true-life stories are vivid and gripping... sometimes humorous and sometimes heart wrenching... giving greater appreciation for the forge that brought forth this hope reformer. You'll be surprised at how this timely and rare message will come alive in you. You'll feel it! It's time! It's time for the whole body of Christ to champion a powerful and triumphant message of hope!

Pastor Bill Johnson
Bethel Church
www.ibethel.org

A Word From Amyann

May our Lord Jesus Christ himself and God our Father,
who loved us and by his grace gave us eternal
encouragement and good hope, encourage your hearts
and strengthen you in every good deed and word.
– II Thessalonians 2:16,17 NIV

Proud To Be His Daughter

I have vivid memories of the first discussion my dad and I had about writing the book you now hold in your hands. Dad was leaning across the table with some handwritten notes scrawled on a napkin. "Just consider coming home for the summer to write books with me," he said. That was his invitation. Mom and Dad were having breakfast with me that morning to discuss my plans for the next several months. It was springtime and I was living in California attending ministry school. Mom and Dad's visit brought the invitation to go on another adventure.

The moment Dad said the words "write books", I broke eye contact with him and began to study the pie display across the room. Images of hours transcribing, writing and rewriting overwhelmed me. But memories also flooded my mind, the stories of Dad's life and our family's journey in hope. Many of the most treasured moments of my life have been spent listening to Dad recount his life's journeys, the humorous tales of his childhood, the trials of his youth, his tender moments with his father, and the victories of his life with God. The idea of writing Dad's journey in hope made my heart leap simultaneously in anticipation and apprehension. Was I ready for this?

It has been my great joy and honor to work with my Dad to capture his journey of hope in God. I have always understood that Dad's history is my inheritance and I have sought to glean all that I can from his life with God. I have come to the realization that Dad's life is much more than just one man's journey; his life is a call for everyone to join a lifelong journey of hope in God. I have taken my dad's story and written this book as an invitation for you to also partake in this inheritance of understanding the God of hope.

For years, Dad has been encouraging me to write a book. He is always pushing me out of my comfort zone and hoping in me beyond my own perceived capabilities. Working on this book has been quite an adventure. I still don't know if I was completely ready for it! I knew putting my Dad's story and heart into words would be quite an undertaking but I was not aware of the results it would produce in my life as we began to write.

As Dad and I began recounting his journey, reviewing his history for this book it was as if our hearts hit another layer of the gold mine in this area of hope. Beyond our wildest dreams and comprehension, we have begun to see in deeper ways how God desires to restore hope to people, cities and even whole nations. It is settled in our spirits, and we cannot let it go. We will reach for this reality of hope for the rest of our lives, and then afterwards.

A Clarion Call To The World

More than a good story, Dad's journey of hope is a clarion call for each one of us to unearth the treasure of hope. It is time for us to start a revolution of hope and tear down the invisible factories inside our souls that produce doubt, cynicism and unbelief and keep us from living life to the fullest.

The Lord is offering His hope to people so they may be free of the voice of disappointment, fear and doubt rattling in their heads. The Lord wants to help people break free from their self-focus and to come into their inheritance of a secure hope in Him. This book records some of the key truths of this journey toward hope.

In this life there will be very challenging times ahead, but God is calling forth patriarchs and matriarchs of hope who will bring forth His hopeful message in the midst of those challenges. The next generation, my generation, must be prepared for the times ahead. They must be given the tools necessary to have hope in God and embrace life even through the most difficult circumstances.

For those of you who feel like you have established some measure of hope in God in your life, I pray that this book will resound within you and build upon your understanding of hope as you become a hope reformer. For those of you who are suffering from hopelessness, doubt, depression or fear, I pray that the message of this book will cut through the layers of oppression in your life and capture your heart. May you be set free by this message of hope in God and become all you were ever meant to be in Him.

Henry Thoreau once commented that most men live lives of meaningless desperation. But this is not our inheritance in Jesus. He came to earth that we might have abundant life (John 10:10). This means that our lives are designed to be encouraged day by day. Hebrews 3:13 (NIV) says, "May your hearts be encouraged while it is still today". Without daily hope, we become dulled by the mundane and wearied by each day's challenges.

There is a desire that originated in the heart of God. This is a desire for people, cities and nations to be brought into an everlasting reality of hope in God. Hope in God is not an option. It is a mandate. Anything less than a message proclaiming the goodness of God is a message that robs the world of true meaning and purpose in life.

What You Will Find

The first section of this book is dedicated to a redefinition of hope. The Lord has taken my dad on a journey to answer the questions of his heart concerning hope. What is hope? And how can we establish hope in every arena of our life? The second section of this book deals with the five pillars of hope, five areas of life the Lord has led our family (and many others) to establish in order to become hope reformers. The last section of the book is an invitation for you to overcome hopelessness and go on the hope journey, becoming a hope reformer who impacts the world with the force of hope.

IS IT NOT YOUR JOURNEY AS WELL?

It's not my goal to have you try to implement another spiritual discipline after reading this book. Instead, I pray you'll respond to the invitation of going on an adventurous journey of hope in God. May the stories of Dad's life stir a longing for true hope in God within you. As you read, please remember that this journey is not just my Dad's journey. It is your journey as well. It is your history of hope. It is your legacy.

A Word From Bob

"...we wait for the blessed hope—the glorious appearing
of our great God and Savior, Jesus Christ."
– Titus 2:13 NIV

Proud To Be Her Dad

It is a tremendous honor to have written this book with my daughter who is not only my daughter, but also my best friend and a leader for me in hope. I do not know if I have ever met anyone more alive in hope or more vibrant towards the positive possibilities of life in God. She is truly becoming a "hope reformer."

In co-authoring this book, the Lord has brought us more understanding and depth than could ever be contained in one book on who He is as the God who is filled with hope and makes everything beautiful just in time. He is our greatest adventure.

Amyann has done an amazing job of crafting my words and story together in a way that is understandable and clear for you, our reader. Her hope in God has shone through every line and it is an invitation for you to go on this journey with us.

DEEPER WATERS OF THE KNOWLEDGE OF GOD

My role in God throughout the years has been to run ahead and scout out for others the territory of God's nature we are to reclaim. I live to see the greatness of His name vindicated in the earth.

A landmark experience in my life launched me on this journey of hope. In 1989, I was the youth pastor of a large church and also led national youth conferences. In the midst of leading the youth, I had a dream that changed the course of my life with God and my ministry. In the dream, I was leading young people into shallow waters of the knowledge of God and it was killing them.

I realized I had not led young people into a deeper part of His nature. I knew I had so much farther to go dive deep into the knowledge of God. I saw "forgotten faces" of God, parts of His nature that had been hidden because we had not been looking. And I knew I must search them out. God instructed me to rid the earth of despair by opening up the knowledge of God and specifically, the knowledge of God in hope.

Shortly after this dream, I met with Bob Jones, a close friend and mentor who showed me the passage in Isaiah 45:3 where it refers to "hidden treasure of the deep." There are treasures in God that have been locked up for hundreds of years. It is time to uncover them.

I have given my life to find this hope in God that is a treasure for all people and will last forever. Scripture tells us that these three realities remain forever: faith, hope and love. Hope is an immortal, indomitable, and eternal truth and it is my lifelong journey.

The Invitation For You

As I continue the adventure of this journey of hope in all of life, I believe I am to call others to this journey as well. Since 1983, I have envisioned cities and nations that would love God well, and thousands of people who would sing the song of wisdom over their cities and nations. The Lord is raising up hope reformers all over the earth and taking them on this journey of hope. He is establishing the force of hope in our lives that will transform cities and nations for His glory.

Together, we are to unlock this golden treasure of hope and fight off the idol of despair. We are to release a true and powerful hope in God that shatters doubt, fear and cynicism, breaking through the clouds of hopelessness with the light of His presence. It is a daily choice to live out a life of hope, but it is the inheritance of every believer.

I would like to issue an invitation to you to come along on the journey. Go on this journey with us to unlock the golden treasure that is true hope in God. The purpose of this book is to unfold the mystery of hope. The journey to unfold this mystery will change your life. All are invited into the knowledge of the God of Hope. Find yourself in this story.

section one

℘

DEFINING
HOPE

chapter one

THE INITIAL INVITATION

Behold, I stand at the door and knock; if anyone
hears My voice and opens the door, I will come in to
him and will dine with him, and he with Me.
— Revelation 3:20

THE CHICAGO HOTEL ROOM IN 1983

It had been a long evening of discussions and debate. I was ready to turn in for the night. As I headed to my hotel room, I met a man at the elevator whose story changed the course of my life.

In 1983, I was a college wrestler and applied the "do it wrong, harder" principle to most areas of my life. A buddy persuaded me to go to a Christian convention in downtown Chicago. The convention was for campus ministry leaders but my friend and I were just there for the travel opportunity.

The other convention attendees were dedicated to the cause of Christ and the ministry of the gospel, but I was as far away from the Lord as I had ever been in my life. They assumed that since I was a part of the convention, I was on the same page regarding spiritual matters. I shocked them all by saying I did not even agree with their basic premises. I was critical and antagonistic of their beliefs in God and challenged many of the students to endless debates about theology.

I grew up in a Catholic environment, and was a loud, obnoxious youth. I was constantly frustrating the nuns, my teachers and anyone who had the unenviable job of trying to restrain me. I showed little regard for rules and regulations and pushed my teachers to the limits of their patience. My history with authority led me to perceive God as severe, distant and altogether frustrated with me because the authorities in my life responded to me in this way.

That evening at the hotel, after I continued my pattern of challenging others to debate and discussion, I headed back toward my room when a gentleman stopped me. He began to share the gospel with me. Ironically, he was not even part of the ministry that was hosting the convention. He was just another hotel guest but he must have felt the Lord's leading to talk to me.

At first I engaged him in conversation, looking for another debate about the nature of God and the purpose of life. But quickly I found this man was different from the others with whom I'd been debating earlier in the evening. This stranger was one of the kindest men I had ever met. He was gentle and sincere and even though he had never met me, I felt as though he loved me and cared deeply for my well-being.

The man shared a heartfelt testimony with me of his salvation and relationship with Jesus. I was greatly impacted by the sincerity of his story. This was not the intellectual debate to which I'd become accustomed. The man described God as a good father who cared for his sons and daughters most intimately and personally. I had never thought of God this way.

I challenged the man as I had often challenged everyone else I knew and yet he answered each of my doubts with a gentle answer that diffused my anger. When I spoke in a way that was not respectful to Jesus, I could tell it hurt him. I was taken back by his genuine love for God. There was no way I could have walked away from the encounter with that man without an impact on my soul.

Even though I was still questioning the goodness of God, I felt this conviction deep within me: if God really was a good Father, He would answer me if I cried out to Him.

After the meeting, I went back to my hotel room and prayed, "If You really are who that man said You are, then I am staying here and not leaving until I meet You as this good Father that he described you to be!" For years the weight of wondering who God really was had pressed upon my soul. In a moment of desperation all my defenses came down. I could no longer ignore this ache for God within me, covering it up with intellect and the reasoning of man. I had to know who He really was and if He truly cared for me.

I began to hope that there was more to God than the picture of a harsh, remote Deity I had experienced while growing up. The man's testimony stirred up a deep desire within me to know a good God and to perceive Him in all of life's circumstances. I had suppressed my desire to know Him; I had buried it underneath the pain and confusion of troubled teenage and young adult years. But all of a sudden it was alive again. I realized that I was "dying from the lack of the knowledge of God" (Hosea 4:6).

I stayed in that room for the next few days, asking the Lord who He was and how He felt about me, leaving only to eat or walk, but all the while thinking of Him. Was God really a good father? Was He really a loving friend? Who was He as creator? Who was He in all areas of life? I had this burning desire to meet the One who had created me and I refused to give up until I encountered Him. I was in desperate need of a true healed and expanded view of the nature of God.

IF GOD REALLY WAS A GOOD FATHER, HE WOULD ANSWER ME IF I CRIED OUT TO HIM.

I knew I had totally underestimated Him. I had pictured Him as the God of the corner of the church but I was desperate to meet the God of all of life. I did not have the understanding or the language for it then, but I ached to see the God who was brilliant in business, the author of education, the one who held a perfect picture of family, the God who had a perfect understanding of true government and ruled in all arenas of life.

God Answered My Perplexity

In my hotel room, my heart was torn and my mind perplexed as I reviewed the tragedies I'd experienced in my life. "Where were You, God, when my mother had several back surgeries and was riddled with pain? Where were You when our family suffered from economic challenges and from emotional problems surrounding my mother's poor health? Where were You when I moved out of my house as a teenager with little means of survival? Where were You then and where are You now?"

My struggle went on for a few days until one afternoon I experienced a breakthrough. I sat on the edge of my bed asking questions of God. Words cannot capture what happened next. Suddenly I knew He was there. I knew He had come. His presence was like a red hue; a burning tenderness filled the room and silenced all my questions.

Everything changed for me that day. His presence answered that deep desire to know who He was. I realized He was not the severe God I had imagined Him to be, but a tender God who was full of love and hope for me. Like the loving embrace of a Father, His presence expressed His deep affection for me. I'd never felt such peace, redemption of my past and hope for my future. These feelings, so foreign to me, were not my own. I knew that this was how God Himself felt about me.

I identified with Job. After wrestling with his friends and his circumstances, Job surrendered to God: "I used to hear of Him with the hearing of the ear, but then I saw Him with the seeing of the eye" (Job 42:5). I no longer just heard of Him. I experienced Him deeply for myself.

I realized that God was the One who loved me enough to die for me. He forgave me of my offensive past. I received the inheritance of His sacrifice: salvation. He was the One who accepted me. He was the one who delighted in me.

He answered me in my distress. I had cried out to Him for days in the hotel room and He met me in an unbelievable way. In that room, I had a revelation that He really was the compassionate and gracious God, slow to anger, abounding in love and faithfulness. I did not deserve His kindness, His mercy or His love. Yet He came.

A New Healed And Expanded View

As I sat in His presence that day, God took me on a journey of redefining my past according to a view of love and hope. He showed me where He had been through the difficulties of my life. He reminded me of scenes from my life and I saw them again, in a new light, as if I was seeing them for the first time.

I remembered when I lived in my car a few years earlier, wondering how I would find food or gas money. Then I remembered how my older brother would slip twenty-dollar bills in the car when I was not around. The Lord said, "That was me". He was behind my brother's kindness, caring for my needs and watching out for me.

I remembered my Dad telling me one Thanksgiving years earlier that I would be quite a man someday. He believed in me even when I had given up all hope on myself, and the Lord said, "That too, was me."

I remembered that when my mother was bedridden and our family was going in so many different directions, I used to sit out on our roof trying to process the perplexities. I remembered how my youngest brother would come sit with me, listen to me, and care for me even when his own needs were being neglected. The Lord said, "That was me."

The Lord showed me countless other scenes where He had worked through a person or an event to bring comfort to me when I desired it most, hope when I lacked vision, and daily provision when I was in need.

I saw how He had been there every moment and I had not recognized Him. I discovered that He was a passionate, pursuing, hope-filled God who had fought for my heart throughout my life.

Not only had He been there in my past, but I could feel that He was invested in my future. Later I would study Jeremiah 29:11 and learn that He is the hopeful God who has an infinite number of plans and dreams for my future, plans to give me a future and a hope.

HE IS THE HOPEFUL GOD WHO HAS AN INFINITE NUMBER OF PLANS AND DREAMS FOR MY FUTURE.

I knew that while everyone on the earth would be partly a stranger, He would be my best friend. My confidant. My comrade. He was the passionate pursuer of my soul, the redeemer of my past, a dedicated Father that would fight for me and most importantly, my best friend, in whom I could hope.

Hearing God's Heart

After I left that Chicago hotel room, I would ask God what was on His heart. Through the following months, we began to develop a deep friendship together where I desired to care for Him, as I knew He cared for me. What was He thinking? What was He feeling? I wanted the things that were important to His heart to become important to mine.

I was persistent in my daily life about asking the Lord what was on his heart. One day, a few months later, I was on a stairwell in my apartment building when the Lord gave me a vision. I saw a collage of vivid pictures of people who were in seemingly hopeless situations – people who were just like me before I encountered the love and hope of God.

I saw the lost who had no hope, young people with no vision for their future, elderly being discarded, and people who had been stripped of their dignity and worth.

My heart was ignited with an unquenchable desire to bring hope to the people who were lost or uncared for; those people, cities and nations that were on God's heart. I knew I had been called to a lifelong journey of obliterating hopelessness in the earth. My heart came so alive with God's call.

chapter two

A NEW DEFINITION
OF HOPE

*Now may the God of hope fill you with all joy
and peace in believing, so that you will abound
in hope by the power of the Holy Spirit. .*
— Romans 15:13

WHAT IS HOPE?

Before the encounter with God in the Chicago hotel room,
I had made some earlier positive decisions for hope in my
life with the help of mentors who demonstrated hope in
God. But I had never experienced for myself the true hope
in God that comes from life with Him.

Though I had had a magnificent salvation experience with
Jesus, I knew I needed to learn to nurture hope in my life.
Neither my life experience nor my education had given me
the tools necessary to cultivate the core human virtues
of faith, hope and love. Though the three are inextricably
bound, I found myself drawn to learn all I could about
hope. I discovered Christ who transformed my hopeless-

ness, and filled me with hope that would transform not only my future, but my past and present as well.

EXPECTATION FOR GOOD

Webster's Dictionary defines hope as "a desire to cherish with expectation of fulfillment; to long for with expectation of obtainment; to expect with desire; desire accompanied by expectation of or belief in fulfillment."

This definition is a helpful starting place, but God's hope expands upon this definition exponentially. Hope is anticipation for good from God in all areas of life. Hope is not a distant or ethereal concept, but a perspective of abundant life that sees and expects good from God to happen in our families, our churches, our businesses, our cities, and our nations.

Hope gives us the ability to carry a supernaturally positive perspective of both our near and distant future. Hope gives us the ability to see a long way out with certainty and confidence in God. Hope is that which enables us to see our children and their children having a good future. Hope enables us to have a wondrous view of eternity. Supernatural hope also means that an eternal perspective fills our present life experience.

A perfect picture of hope is that of children waiting expectantly on Christmas morning before they are given the go-ahead by mom and dad to rush downstairs. They have no doubt their presents are waiting underneath the tree. They pace, laugh and shout upstairs until they are allowed to come bounding down the stairs to meet the goal of their desire.

Paul noted, "Hope is that which does not disappoint because the love of God has been poured out into our hearts" (Romans 5:5). His love is never-ending, and His hope cannot be exhausted as a result. Though our circumstances may be difficult, hope can help us navigate through each challenge, while moving us forward in God. Hope is a strong force that will not bring disappointment.

One Theme – Hope

I will reach for this reality of hope for the rest of my life. I remember the bitterness and hopelessness that consumed my life before I met God. Activities could not fill me. Success could not satisfy me. I had to have a hope in something deeper and truer than what this life had to offer.

My life had little meaning, little clarity, and no true vitality or vibrancy until God opened up the doors for me to see a new future, a new hope, and a new view of life according to His love for me. He gave me a hope I couldn't imagine and didn't deserve. He is the author of my life, my sustainer and my everything.

By the grace of God, I am going to do all that I can to see the next generation given the promises of hope so they do not have to live under the weight of hopelessness. The hopelessness I experienced as a young man, the desperateness of challenging family situations, the emptiness of an ungodly lifestyle, and all the unanswered questions are things I never want to see any person young or old struggle with.

HOPE IS A CARDINAL EXPRESSION OF GOD'S CHARACTER.

Our children have an inheritance of hope that is worth defending and worth laying down our lives for. I refuse to see my children and the people that I am to care for be afraid of a world that is already afraid of the challenges of life.

Hope is not an abstract concept. Hope is a cardinal expression of God's unchangeable character. Scripture tells us that everything except faith, hope and love will pass away (1 Corinthians 13:13). Hope is a treasure that is eternal. It will last beyond the temporal things of this life. Our cultivated faith, hope, and love are the gifts we get to give to the Lord when we stand before Him in eternity. They are the only three things that will remain. They are the only things that will last.

Hope, love and faith, give us the ability to overcome evil with good. Hope is strength, a force from God's very heart. Hope is a substance that comes from Him because He is hope. This calling to proclaim hope cannot be separated from my desire to grow ever closer to Christ. Contagious, life-transforming hope can only be found in Him. It is worthy of a lifetime search because it is the very essence of Jesus, who is the Man of hope.

A Different Picture Of The Future

My father was an inner-city principal and my mother was mostly bedridden for many years with severe back pain.

My family did their best, but times were difficult and I left home early. For a while I lived in my car and had few practical life skills that could help me survive.

My youth was a very challenging time for me. I did not have a relationship with the God of hope to guide me through the everyday circumstances of life.

Now, I am very thankful for the events of my youth. God has redefined the difficult experiences of my youth according to His hopeful view. Healing has come to my perspective of my family and allowed me to see the gifts my parents and others were in my life. I can see now how my dad, my mom and my siblings were always committed to love, giving hope to others despite their own personal pain and challenges.

After a few months of living on the streets, living house-to-house and car-to-car, one of my neighborhood friends and his family took me in for a short time. The family owned a local roofing company and I helped out by tearing off roofs and unloading boxcars. It was hard work but it gave me a great outlet for bottled up energy and anger. The father of the family became like a second father to me.

One day, we were working on a house in a run-down neighborhood and he confided in me. "Bobby, I used to live in this neighborhood." As we walked down the street, he pointed at one house after another, telling me about how this person was in prison or that one had died tragically.

I wondered how he had such a different outcome than the rest of the people who had lived in that neighborhood. I asked him how he had overcome so many obstacles in his life.

He responded, "I guess I just pictured a different future for myself."

He pictured a hopeful future and the possibilities of good that could happen to him in his life versus the possibilities of evil. He pictured a good family and a good career. He pictured himself making an impact for good in whatever community he lived in and served. In my estimation, he had become everything he had dreamed to be and more.

True hope is the ability to envision a different future for yourself and for others, to create a scenario that aligns with hope according to God's view! True hope is so much more than mere wishful thinking or even positive thinking towards the future. True hope is God's view of the future. Wishful thinking is a concept, a strategy and a formula. True hope is a Person, a miracle working Person. True hope is the Person of God. True hope is partnering with His eternal plan of success for you and beginning to believe for it for yourself. I would need this hopeful view in the years to come.

HOPE IS A CHOICE

At age sixteen, I began life guarding at a swimming pool in the inner city. About three weeks into the job, a little boy drowned during one of my shifts. I pulled him from the bottom of the pool, his head dropped back against my shoulder and he died there in my arms. I felt helplessness, disbelief, anger, confusion and sadness all at the same time. The reality of what had just happened settled in my soul like a heavy weight. I was overwhelmed by it.

The city newspaper covered the story with me on the front page. Reporters claimed I was an "uncertified guard" who was responsible for the death of the young boy. Articles published in the paper for the next seven days described me as incompetent and undertrained. These reports deepened my despair.

It was one of the most hopeless times of my life. I saw no future for myself. Everywhere I went, it seemed that people I didn't know were talking about the accident – and about how evil I was. One night in a convenience store, a woman who recognized me from a picture in the paper screamed at me about my negligence. This trauma, grief and regret I faced caused me to shut down and lose any true desire for life.

I felt very alone. Months earlier I had cut myself off from my family and was distant from most of the people in my life who truly cared about me. My friends at the time were superficial and I did not feel I had anyone to turn to so I turned inward, bottling up the confusion and anger.

The boy's family quickly brought a multi-million dollar suit against the city. I was named as a principal in

TRUE HOPE IS THE PERSON OF GOD.

the suit. If the family could prove that I was incompetent, uncertified and negligent they would win millions of dollars. The whole case was an attack on my competency as a lifeguard. In the midst of this pain and pressure, I was close to a nervous breakdown. In the weeks following the incident, I began using drugs and alcohol to numb my pain and silence my inner struggle.

After the suit was filed, the city hired a water safety instructor from New York. He was acclaimed as the number one water safety instructor in the United States. They wanted him to teach me every process possible about swim safety so they could display my abilities and prove to the courts that I had been adequately trained.

At first, I avoided the instructor. I had been living in a state of desperate despair for weeks after the accident. But he came and knocked on my door and persuaded me to take a drive with him.

This swimming instructor was an African-American pastor. He had the visionary personality of Martin Luther King, Jr. But on the day we met, this pastor's dream was more personal. He had a dream for my future. He said, "I am reading the newspaper headlines and I can see that they have already buried you. But I am presenting to you a choice for a great future and a great hope." He could see something in me I didn't believe for myself. He asked me if I would enroll in his 'boot camp', and learn to hope. He gave me an opportunity to make a choice for hope.

Though I was reluctant, I agreed to be mentored by him. Through this difficult experience, my water safety instructor taught me that hope gives us view of the future that advances us beyond the present challenges. I was limping into this season of my life with great loss and despair but God enabled me to come out with strength and hope for the future. Though the tragedy of a loss of life could not be undone, I had a choice about how I would move on with my life.

Because of my instructor's excellent training, I became a water safety instructor. Within months I taught older ladies who were afraid of the water to jump off the high dive. All the local TV stations covered the story. The constant faith of my instructor and this little victory of teaching others to swim sparked a measure of strength and hope in me.

During the trial, the city showed a video of me swimming and because of my training, the family was unable to prosecute me for negligence. The court instead found the family negligent for not watching the boy because there had been signs posted to swim at your own risk. However, at the time of the accident, the press had never reported about those signs.

Although at this time of my life I had not yet made a decision to give my life to God, I had begun to make the choice for hope. I would again fall back into hopelessness before I gave my life to God, but I would never forget the power of making that initial choice for hope.

That choice for hope gave me the strength to go to college, becoming an outstanding student and athlete, a manager at a Ramada Inn during my teen years, to buy my first house as a young man, and to accomplish many things that were naturally beyond my training and capabilities. The decision for hope got me out of bed in the

WE MOVE INTO THE FULLNESS OF GOD BY MAKNG A CHOICE TO BE FILLED WITH HOPE.

mornings. Although it was still a distant understanding, the hope in God that my water safety instructor gave me hooked my soul and propelled me forward.

I have learned that hope is volitional. Hope is a renewed mindset that looks for the positive possibilities in God that might lie ahead. It refuses to partner with misery. I could have stayed in my room for weeks after the drowning accident. Instead someone helped me make the choice for hope. Hope is a choice. Each one of us has the power to choose to embrace hope. We move into the fullness of God by making a choice to be fully filled with hope.

Deuteronomy 30:19 says, "... I have set before you life and death, blessing and cursing; therefore choose life, that both you and your descendants may live." After the drowning accident, this was the choice set before me.

Each one of us can choose life or death, hope or hopelessness. The choice to hope in God is more powerful and permanent than any of our current circumstances, or the circumstances our imaginations can create for our futures. God is a good Father, and our future is secure in Him. In Him we have abundant life.

There is a journey of hope for those who will dare to believe in God's never ending goodness and for those who will move outside of the box of despair even when the challenges are so great. This precious commodity of hope is our on-ramp to the highway of recovery from the pit of despair. The Lord will lift us up from the pit and set our feet firmly upon the rock of hope in Him.

LIVING FROM THE INSIDE OUT

Like both my mentor in my childhood neighborhood and the New York water safety instructor taught me many years ago, hope is not defined by our circumstances. When we make the choice for hope and for a bright future we can begin to live from the inside out. Through true hope in God, we begin to see more with our eyes closed than our eyes open.

Hope is certainly tested by challenges, but our circumstances do not define whether or not we have hope. The true source of our hope is the character and nature of God within us. The apostle Paul says, "Christ in you is the hope of glory" (Colossians 1:27). We can reflect God's nature of hope within us through our own attitude and perspective regardless of the circumstances and obstacles we are facing.

It is a living reality that when you make a decision for hope in God something rises up inside of you, and a force of hope surges through you. It isn't drummed up or an opposite reaction to negativity. It is birthed in you from a seed of God that is already inside you. And it will explode into every arena of your life and deeply impact the way you perceive the circumstances of your life.

Many of us have experienced adversity or unspeakable tragedy. Our lives and circumstances sometimes try to teach us not to hope. In 1987, my wife Terry and I were sent as missionaries by our church to Zimbabwe, Africa to be part of an innovative reconciliation program between a group of white Zimbabweans who desired to live and work with black Zimbabwean believers.

We expected to stay there for a year. We were shocked when our visas were revoked after only five months. We had ten days to pack up and leave the country.

We did not know that the day we left would be our last time to see most of our Zimbabwean friends. A few months later, on November 25th 1987, dissidents arrived in the middle of the night at the farm where we'd lived bringing terror with them. By morning, sixteen of the white Zimbabwean believers had been axed to death, the farm had been pillaged, the buildings had been burned to the ground and the surrounded community was left traumatized and broken.

The news of this attack devastated Terry and I. How could this have happened to the people we had lived with and loved so dearly? We knew there had to be something within us that was greater than our present pain and perplexities if our hearts were going to survive and thrive.

Although we could have shut down from pain and unanswered questions, the Lord showed us the anchor of hope that was inside us because He lives within us. He has led us through a healing process over the past twenty years and has restored hope in our hearts for Zimbabwe. His presence within us is greater than the pain of the tragedy. With a perspective of hope, God is moved to the center of our vision and hopelessness is removed.

A heart satisfied from within by God can anchor us when our circumstances threaten to destroy our hope in Him. An ancient proverb teaches that a good man or woman is satisfied from within. It is the reality of the life of God inside of you that paints the picture of your life on the outside. John 7:38 speaks of the living waters that flow from within us. It is this living reality of Christ, the man of hope inside of us.

Our journey of hope allows us to see that hope is an expectation for good from God despite the present challenges. It is an expectation of good from Him in all arenas of life. Hope redefines our past, gives us a redemptive view of the present, and ensures within us a positive view of the future. Hope is also a choice. Once the choice for hope in God is made, it is developed within us and it becomes a part of us. It is the hope of God inside of us that propels us onward in our journey.

HOPE IS AN EXPECTATION OF GOOD FROM GOD.

chapter three

THE NEED FOR HOPE

Hope deferred makes the heart sick,
but desire fulfilled is a tree of life.
— Proverbs 13:12 NASB

DESPERATE FOR A HUG OF HOPE

My father, the principal of an elementary school in the inner city, applied the power of hope in an unforgettable way one day. He received a call from the local police that a father of one of the students was coming to the school to accost his daughter.

Dad went down to the bottom of the stairwell near the entryway of the cafeteria. He posted himself there just before the lunch hour, watching for the young girl in order to protect her from danger. The police ended up intercepting the father before he reached the school, but something profound happened that day as my dad watched for the little girl at the bottom of the stairwell.

The first child who passed him stopped and spontaneously gave him a hug. The second child did the same. Soon there was a line of children all waiting for a hug before they entered the cafeteria.

After ten minutes of this, the cafeteria manager came out to complain to my dad that none of the children were coming in for their meal. That is, until she saw why. "Look at what is happening! All the children are hugging you then going back in line for another hug!" She observed, "Maybe they need a hug more than they need the food."

My Dad replied in surprise, "Maybe they need both." They agreed the children could receive a hug on the way out. My father went there to protect one child, but ended up celebrating all of them.

Just as those children were hungry for my father's embrace, people of all ages are desperate for a hug of hope. They are desperate for the embrace of a loving Father that insures a confident expectation for good inside their souls.

One man expressing a hopeful view of each child changed the culture of the school that day. This story opened my eyes to the way hope can transform a challenging situation. The Lord is offering transforming hope to each one of us. This hope silences the accusing voices of disappointment, fear and doubt rattling in our heads and hearts. Our inner reality is changed by hope, but this is not where it ends. The atmosphere of an entire school, or even a culture, can experience transformation because of an infusion of God's supernatural hope.

THE IMPACT OF HOPE

Hope brings meaning to those who have lost their ability to look brightly towards the future because of the pain of the past. I experienced the life-changing effects of hope during my years as a public speaking instructor at a university.

We were not allowed to have food or drinks in the classroom but at the end of each semester I would have one of my students watch the door and we would tape up the streamers, pull out the grape juice champagne and chocolate cake and throw a party.

Each student would stand individually, and as a class we would offer that person words of hope and affirmation. Many of these students had never been publicly celebrated but I remembered observing how my dad celebrated his students and I purposed to do the same.

One young man was always very difficult in the classroom. Robert would put down other ethnic groups during class and appeared to find joy in provoking others. It seemed he liked people hating him, and it wasn't hard to do! One day I pulled him out in the hallway and asked him to explain his behaviors.

"Mr. Hartley, I don't know why I act this way," he said, shrugging.

Although it was not normal protocol, I called his family to find out a little bit more of his background. Often at the beginning of each semester, I would ask for the students' permission to call their family members and get more history or background on them if needed. This helped me to understand their needs specifically in order to help them overcome their apprehension towards public speaking.

HE WOULD NOT LET THE PAIN OF THE PAST STEAL HIS VISION FOR THE FUTURE.

When I called Robert's parents, I had genuine concern for Robert and cared to know why he was acting the way he was. They told me Robert's story. "Robert was sitting on our porch one evening. A friend was in the driveway and started backing out the car and did not see Robert's little brother on a tricycle at the end of the driveway. The little boy was killed instantly." Robert had not been the same since that day.

I did not tell the other students what happened, but one day when Robert was not in class, I asked the other students to have a specific encouragement for Robert at our upcoming end of the year celebration. They agreed to do whatever they could to bring Robert into hope.

Ten years later I was in a restaurant having breakfast with my children and felt a tap on my shoulder. It was Robert. Immediately he began to tell my children what had happened to him on our last day of class. "Let me tell you what happened to me that day!" He told the story of how the other students in my class had spoken hope and his true identity to him and he began to believe it about himself. He decided that day that he would not let the pain of the past steal his vision for the future or his love for life or people. He had made a choice for hope.

One little seed of hope planted that day made all the difference for him in his life. He went on to tell me he was running several banks inside of a national grocery store chain. He had responded to the genuine expressions of hope expressed on his behalf, stepping into that door of identity and hope. God's desire is for each of us to respond to the hope He has planted inside of them. This response begins as we bring our past pains and failures before Christ and choose to lean into His hopeful perspective.

God does not want us to be living in a hopeless state; He wants us to be fully alive! He cares that we move forward in love and hope into this season of our lives. We are more than conquerors through Him when we receive a vision of hope

Pillars Of Hope

In 2008, I had a life-changing dream about "five pillars of hope." In the dream, these five pillars were a significant part of seeing cities, nations, cultures, and societies transformed. Hope is meant to be the foundation of our lives. These five pillars rise from the foundation of hope.

My dream was of a heavenly classroom and the subject was God's hope. The teacher, Jesus, took me and other hope reformers back through our own personal journeys of hope in Him. He showed me how I had progressed in hope without fully recognizing it. I learned that I was never to underestimate the value of my personal life's journey in hope. It was vital to my understanding of His orchestration of hope in my life so that I could stay in a position of hope and show others where He had been there for them as well. My hope journey created golden keys for the sake of others. There was a synchronizing of my life events and hope memorial stones that were for the common wealth of people who decided to go on the journey of hope. He was calling everyone to this journey.

WE ARE MORE THAN CONQUERORS THROUGH HIM WHEN WE RECEIVE A VISION OF HOPE.

Then He offered me an invitation to continue on this royal journey of hope by establishing these five pillars in my life. The five pillars are Hope In God, Hope In Prayer, Hope In People, Hope In The Next Generation, and Hope In Cities And Nations. The five pillars were like rows in the classroom. The other students and I had to pass the life lessons of each of the five pillars in order to graduate into hope. We were seated in each row and taken through a process of making a decision to view our life lessons according to God's perspective of hope in these five pillars of hope.

In the dream I advanced through each row, one at a time with the help of my instructor, Jesus, who was the Man of Hope. In the dream, I knew that upon graduation, I would be commissioned to proclaim a message of hope to the world along with other hope reformers – those who impact the lives of others, as well as our cities and nations with the force of hope in God.

There was a great coronation for those who had graduated the class and had committed to establish each of the five pillars of hope in their lives. Upon graduation, these hope reformers were able to usher in great clouds of hope over cities and nations, dispelling clouds of despair and doubt advancing onward with hope. The dream ended with that picture of clouds of hope resting over the nations raining down with the glory of hope in God.

I saw the transforming power of hope in the life of my former student, Robert. If one little seed of hope could change his life, what could five pillars of hope do? Living our lives from a place of being established in these hope pillars enables us to become hope reformers to change cities and nations.

FIGHTING THE GIANT OF DESPAIR – HOPE WINS

One of the greatest enemies of love and life in our generation is the enemy of hopelessness. Like David going out to fight the Philistine giant (I Samuel 17:4, 32), we may feel weak and small compared to such an intimidating enemy.

When David went to meet the giant Goliath, he chose five small stones as his weapons. Like David's five stones, I believe God has given us five pillars of hope for us to develop in our lives once we make the decision for hope.

The decision to hope and to fight the giant of despair is inseparable from the decision to follow Christ. He is the God of hope. Many people make a decision to follow Christ without a full understanding of Him and His nature. It is easy to have a wrong image or incomplete image of God but it is time to walk in the fullness of this Christian life by overflowing in hope and destroying despair - the enemy of hope!

What Are These Five Pillars?

Hope In God

Hoping in God allows us to see Him as near and present in our everyday lives. Hoping in God opens us up to a brilliant discovery of the Son of God as the One who deeply cares for us. When we have hope in Him, we learn to believe He is able to turn our doubts and fears about the future into a place of expectation in Him. Hope in God expands our view of who God is. We see Him not as the "God living in the corner of the church," anymore, the One who is limited to just our church experience, but as the "God of all of life"!

Hope In Prayer

The pillar of Hope In Prayer restores trusting, intimate friendship with God as we commune with him in our daily lives. Hope In Prayer also enables us to build and advance life on our knees in a place of prayer.

Hope In People

Hope In People allows us to see one another through God's eyes. We begin to see people with the eyes of Jesus according to their greatness and capabilities instead of their perceived incapacities. Hope In People enables us to speak life into them, inviting them into the beauty of their destinies in God.

Hope In Cities And Nations

Hope In Cities And Nations is nothing less than a Kingdom vision of the world God loves. We see lands through the eyes of hope. This understanding changes the way we pray for and interact with those in our town or on the other side of the globe.

Hope In The Next Generation

Hope gives us the opportunity to lend a hand and a plan to the next generation by believing in them and fighting for their future. It enables us to see them with the redemptive eyes of God and call forth the beauty and purpose He has given them.

Enter The Journey

There is a beautiful invitation for each one of us to devote our lives to discover the limitless hope within the Man, Christ Jesus. Through my life, I have discovered that each one of us has a great call to walk into hope as a hope reformer. As hope reformers, we are invited to establish these five pillars of hope in our lives through the help of our Lord, Jesus. It is the foundation upon which hope reformers build their lives.

TREASURES OF HOPE ARE STILL TO BE DISCOVERED.

God desires us to walk confidently experiencing the adventure of each day in Him. In Him there are pleasures forevermore. Treasures of hope are still to be discovered to give people back their life, their vision, their purpose. For me, mining out this treasure has not been just a dramatic call but a lifelong journey.

Just as I learned that hope could transform a school lunch period – or the despair of a young man who had witnessed his brother's death, I believe that hope can transform every aspect of our lives. My dream of the hope reformers allowed me to begin to understand that as I mined the treasures of the deep, these treasures became a part of my ministry to establish hope. These treasures belong to you, too. They can help you establish hope in your own life in each of the "five pillar" areas. The next section of this book will describe the five pillars of hope.

section two

&

THE FIVE PILLARS OF HOPE

chapter four
PILLAR 1: HOPE IN GOD

No one who hopes in You will ever be put to shame.
— Psalm 25:3 NIV

HE IS ENOUGH

Before my wife Terry and I left for mission service in Zimbabwe in 1987, we were honored with a round of gatherings designed to send us off with love. In the midst of the festivities, a prophetic brother, Bob Jones, confronted me. He told me not to go to Africa or to take Terry. His concern and harshness caught me completely off guard in the midst of all the celebration. He said that people were going to die there in Zimbabwe and I would be a fool to go to such a dangerous place. "If you want to go, then go, but don't take 'tender Terry' to her death," He warned. I did not appreciate his words or his approach.

As it grew nearer to our departure date, several other important people in our lives pointed out the volatile state of the country and warned us not to go at that time. We went in spite of the warnings.

On the long journey to Africa, a sense of aloneness gripped me. What had we gotten into? The moment we stepped into Zimbabwe I could feel the insecurity of the nation. I could see fear behind the eyes of the people and feel the growing sense of the panic of a nation in disarray.

The leaders of the community in which we were going to live met us at the airport. Instead of fanfare and excitement, our meeting was solemn and serious. We rode in silence most of the way to the farm where the community was located. As we got closer, the leaders began to inform us of the growing danger the community was facing.

They explained that a few nights before we had arrived a local group of dissident terrorists who opposed the racial reconciliation work of the community had threatened the lives of those living on the farm. They had rounded them up in a circle and danced around them, screaming for their blood. They stole their clothing and electronics and left them with threats of further terrorism. These terrorists had been creating regular disturbances over the past months, stirring up fear and unrest amongst the members of the community.

In light of the situation, Terry and I were encouraged by the leaders of the community to seek the Lord and decide whether to stay in Zimbabwe as planned or get on an airplane and head back to the US. Still in a state of shock, we did our best to seek the Lord's will and weakly decided to stay in Zimbabwe.

Once we arrived at the farm, we quickly saw for ourselves that the situation was escalating. The danger was at a much higher level than we thought. In the following weeks, the dissidents began attempts in the middle of the nights to pillage the farm and burn it down.

The frequency of attacks and threats increased. Often we would find that our chickens had been stolen in the middle of the night and threats had been painted on the fencepost that the dissidents were planning to kill us all. We took turns at night lying in the bush keeping watch in an attempt to stop them or catch them.

Though my heart was quickly joined to the people of Zimbabwe and especially to the other members of the community on that farm, I carried a sense of shame and confusion that I'd refused to listen to the warnings of wise people prior to our departure from the U.S. I was used to having my own zeal, strength and sense of duty carry me through difficult situations. But I knew my own self-strength would not be enough this time.

God used those early days in Zimbabwe to tutor me about my own weakness. I faced my own inadequacy and need for God. I quickly discovered that hope in God alone would be the single way in which I could access His strength in order to face the challenges ahead and protect my wife.

I COULD ACCESS HIS STRENGTH IN ORDER TO FACE THE CHALLENGES AHEAD.

One of my jobs on the farm was to chop wood each day. I would go up on a hill and chop wood for hours. There I began to try to process my concern for our future with God. I prayed as I chopped: "Please give us what we need from You, Lord. My zeal won't do it this time. Only love from You and hope in You can carry Terry and I through whatever comes here in Zimbabwe."

I expected that I'd need to expend additional energy to drill deep in order to discover His strength, but my weakness and surrender drew Him near. I could feel His tender love and His hopefulness for my future. His protection was complete. I knew we were safe. I felt as though I was living in the valley of the shadow of death, but I was closer to Him than I had ever been and His presence was as exhilarating as it was comforting. It was like I walked as though I walked on butter and it reminded me of Job's declaration, "my steps were bathed in butter, and the rock poured out for me streams of oil!" (Job 29:6 NASB).

When I began not to worry like a man, but to trust like a child, the ceiling that separated me from the knowledge of hope in God came crumbling down. The result of love and simple faith in God brought a deep confidence in Him. I knew, whatever happened, God would care for us.

My repentance over my headstrong decision-making and my self-reliance placed me in a classroom that allowed me to learn moment by moment how real and tangible his hope was. Our circumstances had not changed, but I was encountered with such hope that was the very substance of God. I had found my hope in Him.

It was amazing what happened in the following months amongst the people of the community. As we faced the challenges of everyday life together while existing with the reality of ever-present danger, we went to a deep place of friendship with one another and a true reliance upon God. He released to us a supernatural hope in Him that surrounded us everyday. I remember some beautiful moments of worship and prayer together, as well as some tender times of vulnerability as we all faced the same danger. We knew that God was bigger than the circumstances and even in the midst of a very trying situation He still would love and care for us.

After five months of living in the community, Terry and I went to the embassy for a regularly-scheduled appointment to have our visas updated. We had each a two-year visa but for some reason at the five-month mark the Zimbabwean officials revoked our visas. We were told to leave the country immediately. We were shocked and confused and very torn.

We experienced a mix of feelings as we got ready to leave Zimbabwe. We wanted to stay with the ones there that we had grown to love, but were ready to leave the constant danger. We knew that the lives of those we loved were still in danger and it was hard to leave them.

Because we had been planning on a much longer stay overseas, Terry and I were not ready to go back to U.S. yet. We had few resources, and decided to head to Israel to live and work on a kibbutz for several months.

On Thanksgiving evening, one week after retuning home to Kansas City, a dear friend from South Africa, Noel Alexander, arrived at our home. Noel told us that the other members of the community that we had lived with in Zimbabwe had been taken into a room and had been axed to death one by one by the dissidents.

Noel shared that as they were being killed, each person expressed great hope in God. They looked to each other and said, "We are going home tonight." Unmoved in their faith, they had found it. They had found true hope in God that was beyond every challenge and every terrifying reality. They found a hope in God that was even stronger than death itself.

Terry and I felt outrage, anger and deep, deep sense of loss at the news of the death of our friends. But greater than our pain was a hope in God that had been rooted deeply inside of us. I had learned to begin to hope in God on that hill in Zimbabwe and it carried me through the pain and perplexities.

Hoping In His Provision

Hope in God is the most secure, solid place from which to live – no matter how fractured, dangerous or confusing our circumstances may be. He is more committed to our own good than we could ever be.

Hoping in His supremacy means that we can have confidence that He is more than enough for whatever challenge may come own way. The curveballs of life may come, but we can live with the assurance that He is enough in the midst of them.

In Zimbabwe, I met the God who I could hope in for my life and the life of my family. Later, I would learn to trust and hope in God as the one who would meet my day-to-day needs and bring provision for me. A few years ago, I made some large investments with a Christian group involved in buying and selling imports. Several other business and ministry friends had partnered with this group. We were very excited about the investment because we were making solid returns and the group was giving a substantial amount of its profits to the poor. Or so we thought.

The whole thing was a fraud. There was no product being sold and little money was going to the poor. All the stolen money was lost and the individuals responsible went to prison. Along with the loss of the money, there was a loss of hope and the vision of a righteous business venture. In the midst of the confusion, I cried out to God for another level of hope in Him as the God of supply. He answered me in a dream.

I dreamed that I was standing on the outer edge of a kingdom. I had come to the kingdom bearing the weight of my failures in business, feeling that even God's provision was not enough for this situation. My situation exposed my error. I had hoped in the world for supply and to provide for us in our life. Since Zimbabwe,

HOPE IN GOD IS THE MOST SECURE, SOLID PLACE FROM WHICH TO LIVE.

I had trusted in God to preserve my life but not necessarily in His supremacy and ability to care for me above all the issues of life. I had not yet learned to trust in Him for provision.

In the dream a sage came to the window from the place where God dwelled and said, "It is a peripheral issue on the outside of the kingdom, and it doesn't change a thing. The Sovereign God has His Sovereign will for your life and your family and this matter doesn't change a thing about His plan for your life."

In Isaiah 36, Hezekiah had placed his trust in Egypt for military protection and provision. "Look now, you are depending on Egypt, that splintered reed of a staff, which pierces a man's hand and wounds him if he leans on it" (Isaiah 36:6 NIV). Like Hezekiah, I made the error of leaning on the world for provision and it was like placing my trust upon a reed that splintered beneath my weight and pierced my hand. I was not hoping in God, my true provider.

I replied to the sage, "Really? God is enough for my $300,000 loss? He is enough to redeem this situation and bring supply?"

The sage responded, "You are to be a king of supply and not a pauper. The Sovereign God will have a sovereign way and this issue doesn't change a thing. He is your strong tower. He is your impenetrable shield. He is your God of supply. He is the God of provision. He will care for you."

I realized He was the God who was able and willing to provide and I could hope in Him in these circumstances. Although I was inwardly torn and flawed, He was able to redeem my messes and it did not change a thing about His plan for us and His plan to bring provision to others through us. I understood that this failure was not fatal.

My failures were not the story being written in my life. The story was that God was over all, and was able to transform my circumstance for my good and His glory and He would provide for us. "In this world you will have tribulation and trials and distress and frustration; but be of good cheer! For I have overcome the world" (John 16:33 AMP). I discovered that He is so much bigger than the issues of life, big or small!

HE IS SUPREME OVER ALL

In February 2008, I had an intense encounter with the Lord that gave me a glimpse of the scope of what it means to hope in His supremacy. Words are inadequate to capture the glory of this encounter, but the images He showed me have profound implications for all of us as we explore what it means to hope in Him.

I saw the Lord Jesus standing before me and in the palm of His hand was resting everything on the earth. There in His hand, He held all of the earth's governments and economies, and global issues such as abortion and terrorism. In His hand, He also held each and every person on earth. He carried each person's past, present and future. Finally, I saw all of the stars and galaxies of the universe shrink to fit His hand. He holds it all in His hand!

In His supremacy, God carries all the burdens of the world, big and small. He is bigger than the issues. He is enough for every need and every life circumstance. We can hope and trust in Him.

Hoping In His Forgotten Faces

As I learned what it meant to hope in God, I discovered my view of Him expanded exponentially. As I have purposed to lay aside my former view of God, which was defined by my own limited perceptions, I have enjoyed my growing sense of wonder at who He is. I see the entire world tinted by His glory. I have gone from a "portal view" of God – a narrow view defined by my own beliefs and perceptions, to a "big, blue, wide-open-sky" view of God. As King David said, "He brought me out into a spacious place; he rescued me because he delighted in me" (Psalm 18:19 NIV).

He has purposely hidden so many facets of His glory for us to discover. He has invited us to search out his limitless attributes. His face of wisdom, His joyful face, His tender face, His approachable face in everyday life. This brings our hearts into true hope!

There is a great unveiling of these "forgotten faces" of God – aspects of God's nature that have yet to be fully discovered. While there are still many who have not fully forgotten these facets of God, there is so much more of them to be discovered. We have forgotten that there is so much more to search out in the depths of the nature of our God. "It is the glory of God to conceal a matter, the glory of kings to search it out" (Proverbs 25:2 NIV).

A DEEPER UNDERSTANDING OF THE NATURE OF GOD

In the early days of my walk with Christ, I had a dream that completely changed the way I approached life and ministry. In the dream I saw that the youth of this nation and all kinds of people across the world were diving into "shallow waters" of the knowledge of God and it was killing them! They did not know how to dive into the deep richness of the knowledge of the nature of God.

The reason they were choosing the shallow waters was because they had thought that was all there was to who He was. They were not aware that there was more and they weren't equipped to dive into His depths. This dream sent me into a search for a deeper understanding of the knowledge of God for myself. I realized I myself had barely scratched the surface of exploring the attributes of God. I couldn't ask those to whom I was ministering to learn to dive deep until I had gone there first.

HIS NATURE ROOTED HOPE DEEPLY WITHIN ME.

As God began teaching me about His nature, my hope deepened. Through the years I have seen the face of God as a redemptive God, a providing God, a building God, a wise God and many other faces. I saw the unfolding of His nature and goodness and it rooted hope deeply within me.

I saw the Lord's forgotten face as a shepherd when we first began building a small business shortly after I had the dream about the forgotten faces of God. I quickly discovered I was good at only a few aspects needed to successfully run a small business. Terry and I prayed, "Lord, we need a shepherd." I needed someone to guide me through the unknown territory.

Solomon inquired of the Lord, then God came to him as a shepherd and led him to build a great kingdom (I Kings 10). I hoped in a Shepherd God who would lead me in the same way. We knew He could do the same for our business and family, and that He would shepherd us and establish both our family and business in a way that would glorify His name.

I remember as we prayed for Him to shepherd us, He would guide us in our decision-making in the business. Even though I was only good at a few aspects needed to run it, the Lord sent me experts in the areas I was weak. He sent us an excellent accountant. He brought someone to help manage personnel. He would send me the help we needed without us even looking for people to fill the position, sometimes before we even perceived the need for it. It was His perfect guidance.

As we continued this discovery of the forgotten faces of God, hoping in Him caused us to discover another aspect of His nature in our business. We experienced the Son of God as a joyful One, and we learned that it is His nature to celebrate. With His divine guidance the business had begun to grow and grow, but I quickly discovered that sometimes bigger is not always better. With greater success our team was encountering greater problems. We were no longer enjoying the business.

As a staff, we began to proclaim God as the joyful God in business and in the specific areas that were a burden to us. The whole business changed and the atmosphere was filled with life. We stopped focusing on the problems and started rejoicing in our victories. Moments of belly laughing came back. We found this brilliant truth that God is the One who eternally laughs and has great delight. "Therefore God, Your God, has anointed You with the oil of gladness more than Your companions." (Psalm 45:7) Jesus was happier than any other man that has ever lived on the earth and we were able to follow in His footsteps even in the midst of the challenges of a business!

The Lord has revealed Himself as the better-than God with a better-than plan for me many times through my life. One of these times was also through the business. As the business grew, we needed infrastructure. We needed creative ideas for problem solving. We sought the Lord in prayer and He gave us a different way to structure and organize our cleaning business that was better than our current system and enabled us to build our company with a whole lot more efficiency. We invited Him in, hoped in Him and He blessed us.

The Lord has showed me His redemptive face many times through my business. Even in the midst of my business mistakes or in challenging economic situations, God has come forth on my behalf with His redemptive plan. At one point, our cleaning business almost had shut down because a major client was going bankrupt and closing seven locations that were cleaning. But God redeemed the situation for our company and we were able to buy the foreclosed properties. We began a commercial real estate business. This opened many doors for us and enabled supply to be sustained for many families.

The Lord has continued to reveal to me specific aspects of His nature as I have walked the journey of searching them out in everyday life. He loves to be discovered and there are limitless faces of God yet to be discovered in all arenas of life.

HOPING IN HIS UNCONDITIONAL AFFECTION

So much of what I've learned about the depth and richness of having a sustaining hope in the eternal God began during the early days of our time in Zimbabwe. I remember recounting my shame to the Lord in prayer for my insistence in bringing my beautiful wife halfway across the world, jeopardizing her safety but His forgiveness and conditional affection is so complete. He has overlooked my faults and forgiven my sins, instead pursuing me with perfect, joyful love.

Even though King David made many mistakes through His life, he still proclaimed that God was for him. David's strength wasn't defined by his successes or limited by his failures. His strength came from his hope in God. Despite his many weaknesses, he was confident that God was FOR him. In return for our mistakes, God gives us His unconditional love and affection.

David had many astounding failures: moral failures, and unwise decisions that cost people their lives. He did not always operate out of faith, hope and love; many times he was motivated by fear, and self-preservation. Yet Acts 13:22 refers to David as a man after God's own heart who served the purpose of God in His generation. God's affection for David went beyond any failure he had committed.

As I worked through my own failures while chopping cord after cord of wood in Zimbabwe, I experienced wave after wave of God's love and grace, His forgiveness and His hope for my future in Him. Everything within me wanted to crawl away from this unconditional love. I did not feel deserving of this kind of kindness.

The truth was, I didn't deserve it. But my surrender to Him allowed me to

DAVID'S STRENGTH CAME FROM HIS HOPE IN GOD.

receive what He couldn't help but offer to me. It was an expression of His character. He is searching for those who will simply receive the love He has to give them.

There is no one who is worthy; "for all have sinned and fall short of the glory of God, and all are justified freely by his grace through the redemption that came by Christ Jesus" (Romans 3:23,24 NIV). Once we get past the fact that we do not deserve His love and never will, we can begin to accept it. I want to excel at being loved by God, this brings our hearts great hope!

Giving Him Back The Love He Is Due

Not only do I want to be loved well by God, but I long to love Him back by worshiping Him and hoping in Him all throughout the day. God has given us unique forms of worship that are as unique as each one of us. We all have our own unique way of giving back to Him the love that He is due. Our true worship focuses our hearts on Him and gives us hope.

On the farm in Zimbabwe, I met a man named Barnafas. Together we would shovel sand to mix with water for a concrete solution needed to lay the foundation for a dairy that the community was building. Although he was probably half my size, he would shovel twice as much as I. Everyday I would put a little more effort into the job, shoveling faster and harder in an attempt to outwork this little African man. Every day he would shovel more sand than I did.

I grew increasingly frustrated until one day, I couldn't stand it any longer. I grabbed him and tossed him into the pile of sand he'd just shoveled. "How can you shovel like that?" I yelled.

His eyes wide, he replied, "This is my worship."

Barnafas rose from the pile, dusted himself off with great dignity, and invited me to walk to the crest of a nearby hill. He pointed at a man gardening with his son in the small valley below. "That is their worship," he said.

Barnafas did not have to be preaching or prophesying or completing a list of spiritual activities in order to encounter God. He was able to meet and hope in the God of work and industry everyday while he shoveled sand.

It is tempting to limit our definition of worship to the songs we sing or the prayers we pray. This is not how God defines worship, and neither should we. Barnafas' example showed me a primary purpose behind work and everyday life; that it is worship and an opportunity to hope in God in all of our life's activities. This understanding gave all of my life's duties meaning in God.

There are so many forms of hoping in God and encountering God's powerful presence in everyday life. God Himself is so multi-faced. Lydia was a maker of purple. Joshua was a general of an army. Daniel was a governor. Paul was a tent-maker. The ultimate reward of all of our lives is friendship with God. Each day's success is based on the discovery of His presence and how much we were able to enter into communion with Him by hoping in Him in everyday life. This is our great adventure; to experience God and hope in Him in all of life.

The Beauty Of Hoping In Him

We hope in God because He is worthy of our hope, our trust, and our

> WE HOPE IN GOD BECAUSE HE IS WORTHY OF OUR HOPE, OUR TRUST, AND OUR LOVE.

love. He died that we may be able to receive His love and enter into a relationship with Him that secures our hope in Him.

He is our All in All and His supremacy is enough for us to move forward confidently in life. As I experienced on the Zimbabwe hill, hopelessness lifted and there was a hope that came and a new perspective that came through the power of God's presence. Hoping in God brings un-intelligible peace in all of life and we become aware of His presence in our deep center. When we hope in God we allow Him to come meet us in our challenges with all His goodness.

His forgotten faces and the vast aspects of His nature are revealed to us as we begin to hope in Him and search Him out. We begin to find Him in our businesses, our families, our churches and our daily activities.

The unfolding of God's affection is apparent as we let go of our perceived unworthiness and allow Him to love us. Love and hope in God is our inheritance for every mo-ment, every challenge, and every day-to-day activity. In trials and triumphs of everyday life we have the opportu-nity to hope in God and establish the most important of the pillar of hope.

chapter five

Pillar 2: Hope In Prayer

Be joyful always; pray continually; give thanks in all
circumstances, for this is God's will for you in Christ Jesus.
— 1 Thessalonians 5:16-18 NIV

The Warehouse

In 1983, Mike Bickle invited me to join his church staff.
I had an organizational degree and I had a lot of hustle
to build and create. I believed I could help him develop
an internal infrastructure for the church, which is why I
assumed he hired me. There had been great growth in the
church over a short period of time and my education and
experience was in the area of building large organizations
and organizational structures. However, when I asked him
about my job description, he told me my main responsibility was to be on my knees three times a day in prayer.

At that time, the church's prayer room was an old paint
warehouse. It was a silent, cold place with a concrete floor

and walls. The walls were lined with boxes and storage items. It was not an inviting setting.

I was assigned to three two-hour slots of prayer a day. Six hours a day in the warehouse! I was sure Mike had severely missed my potential but I agreed to follow his instructions anyway because I respected his leadership and somehow I felt drawn to what he was asking me to do.

I did not make it to every assigned prayer slot during the week. When I did, I would soldier through my time restlessly. I believed I was wasting my potential and what I could accomplish by spending my time in the prayer warehouse and not building or producing. I felt like a racehorse in the stall. I was ready to get out there and run and win a big race for God and produce great things for His kingdom.

However, I decided I'd try to make the most of this prayer time in the warehouse and I began to explore the promises of the Bible concerning prayer. I focused on the promises of God, exploring His heart on this subject, month after month until one day everything changed. His presence would engulf me as I pondered Him and His promises. I realized I never wanted to leave this place. Just as a racehorse needs to undergo training to run his best, I needed to learn to run – by kneeling, by surrendering, by encountering God in this place of prayer. It was in this place that I discovered the eternal endurance of the second pillar of hope: hope in God through prayer.

HOPE PRAYER IS FRIENDSHIP WITH GOD

On my knees I began to discover that prayer was true friendship with God. I experienced friendship with God that I never even thought was possible.

By His grace, I moved into a place of depth of communion through prayer, which is intimacy with Him. Friendship with God through prayer had been a concept I understood, and therefore, since I had the concept, I thought I was doing it. But suddenly I truly understood what it was like to commune with Him. His friendship with me was more real to me than anything I had ever experienced; His thoughts and feelings were nearer to me than my own.

In this place of friendship with God, I could dialogue with God about anything and everything, enjoying Him and doing life together.

To me the word "prayer" can have connotations of work, effort, and duty. But it is simply friendship with our Father. My initial restlessness when Mike required me to spend so much time in the prayer room was transformed by simply learning to enjoy the friendship of God. Prayer was not just part of my job description. It was life together with my nearest and dearest Friend.

This type of relationship creates hope and confidence in the act and lifestyle of prayer where we go from desperate prayers to confident, hope filled prayers. I knew that because He loved me, He would interact with me and answer my heart's cries. Even earthly fathers love to give good gifts to their children; how much will our Father act on our behalf when we live in communion with Him? (Matthew 7:9-11)

HOPE PRAYER RESTORES OUR CONFIDENCE IN GOD

Prayer moved me from self-dependency to total dependency and trust in God. For me, prayer was a statement of my humble need for God as my source and my strength and in Him I can find answers and resources, instead of looking first to myself.

Before spending time in the warehouse, I had the image in my mind of me carrying the globe on my shoulder while God was in the background watching me carry it for Him.

I was trying to help Jesus by using my own self-strength and perceived multi-talented gifts.

But once I encountered God through prayer, I discovered I was just a simple child. The Lord showed me how to take the globe of perceived responsibility off my shoulders and hand it to Him, and together we would dance on it. He made it clear that the only way I would "do" anything for God was by loving Him, enjoying Him and getting on my knees and inviting Him and His strength into the situation with a hopeful heart in His goodness.

THE ONLY WAY I WOULD "DO" ANYTHING FOR GOD WAS BY LOVING HIM.

I had been desperately trying to paddle down the river of life, moving forward in my own strength. But God showed me how to put the oars inside the boat and put up the sail. God's presence would be the wind in my sails and guide me down the wide canal of a hopeful journey in His will.

In that warehouse, I went from focusing on building my potential as the answer for meeting the needs of the day, to living in His presence and seeing that the answers for life's needs could come forth through the place of prayer. In those times of prayer I learned, I could enjoy Him and rest in the power of hope filled prayer, no longer having to merely trust in my own ability to war with my own strength. Now I simply focus on worshiping Him who is able to win in all circumstances instead of striving on my own.

There were times in my life when it seemed I could not go a minute without having an anxious thought because I was so focused on creating solutions for myself and for the people around me. But entering into communion with a hopeful God through prayer, I can have a confident expectation that He will be my answer.

HOPE PRAYER IS OUR PRIMARY BULIDING METHOD

All of a sudden I realized why Mike had called me to the warehouse. The primary position from which I was supposed to help build the ministry was on my knees. Mike wasn't interested in my organizational methods as much as he was interested in building my prayer life so I could minister out of the fullness of a hope-filled, humble friendship with God. He knew it was not my organizational skills that would move mountains; it was my faith and dependency in God through a place of prayer.

God desires to give us the nations and everything we asked for in His name through prayer and communion with Him. "Ask of me, and I will make the nations your inheritance, the ends of the earth your possession" (Psalm 2:8 NIV).

Jesus gives his final message to His disciples in John 13-17. Nine times He instructs His disciples to "ask". "You may ask me for anything in my name, and I will do it" (John 14:14). He said, "Ask and you will receive, and your joy will be complete" (John 16:24 NIV). In this place of prayer we have great influence to build and create.

As I studied the Word in the warehouse, I began to see how others who had gone before me had learned to build on their knees. Daniel, a governor of a kingdom, set aside three times a day to pray and seek the Lord. King David said seven times a day he stopped to praise Him. Samuel was a judge and ministered to God day and night, talking to Him.

They had cultivated a place of prayer because they knew there was a place of power in prayer to build and manage whole kingdoms.

Solomon also built a kingdom on his knees in prayer. In I Kings 10 the queen of Sheba came and awed at his ability to manage a kingdom, he had such stunning capacity and ingenuity. She saw all the wisdom of Solomon and the palace he had built, the food on his table, the seating of his officials, the attending servants in their robes, his cupbearers. Then she looked at his ascent, the stairwell where he went up to the temple of the Lord to inquire of Him on his knees and she was breathless. Prayer was the source of his ingenuity and wisdom, his ability to manage a whole kingdom better than anyone had ever done before.

THERE IS NO GREATER PLACE FOR INFLUENCE THAN THE PLACE OF PRAYER.

I knew something had changed in me when, after a few months in the prayer warehouse I found myself praying, "I will never leave this place. Here is where my identity is secured in friendship with God and my confidence is restored in Him. Here is where my greatest power and authority is found."

Building on my knees through prayer has been the pattern for my life since then. Both in my family and in the businesses I run, prayer is our primary building "strategy". At different points in my business I have had business challenges. I have asked the Lord how to solve these problems. The answer is always "on your knees."

For instance, a while ago, I was struggling with how to grow my business. I brought my concerns to the Lord, "God, how do I develop our sales force? I have people that are more administrative, but not people who are selling and taking territory. How do I learn to manage them?"

He responded, "On your knees." The Lord reminded me that I needed to begin and end by placing myself before Him, being with Him, and listening to Him. There is no greater place for influence and strength than the place of prayer where we are united to God and completely dependent on Him.

Seeing More With Our Eyes Closed
Than Our Eyes Open

When we hope in God through prayer and communion with Him, we begin to see more with our eyes closed then our eyes open. We begin to see what God dreams and have an infusion of hopeful vision for what is on His heart.

My wife Terry is one of my greatest hope heroes. She truly sees more with her eyes closed than here eyes opened. She responds with courage and vision in the midst of hopeless situations like few people I've ever known. She is a champion of hopeful prayer.

The Lord has given her a gift to see a hopeful future for the most adverse circumstances. Terry has an incredible heart for the people of Zimbabwe.

With the deaths of our friends in Zimbabwe over twenty years ago came the death of a vision for Terry and me. We believed we had witnessed the death of our connection with Africa. However, Terry continued to pray for the peace of Zimbabwe.

God gave Terry a dream a few years ago about "mission possible." In the dream the Lord gave her an invitation to undertake a mission to send a container of supplies to Zimbabwe.

The nation was now in total economic and political ruin. Despite the tremendous level of opposition from a corrupt government, the 40 ft container arrived bringing food and supplies to orphans and believers who were in desperate need.

She is currently involved in launching a program to provide aid for the education of children who have been orphaned by Zimbabwe's unrest. God has given Terry a revelation of hope for the nation of Zimbabwe as she has interceded for the country. Only in the place of hopeful prayer could someone receive vision like she has for such trials and only from a place of prayer can miracles come forth to accomplish them.

My Aunt May

As I look back through the years, I see where God has changed my life through the impact of hopeful prayer. My Aunt May was also one who saw more with her eyes closed than her eyes open and she prayed unceasingly for me through my teenage drug years and times of difficulty.

She was an elderly woman and was called "camel knees," because she had calluses from spending so much time on her knees in prayer. Aunt May never married. She faithfully sought God each day of her life. Her prayer life helped her love us well. At one point during my own stormy teenage years, she opened her home to me and took me in.

One night, I came home so drunk I couldn't make it up the steps so I lay under the bushes next to the porch. She did not know I was home, so she sat on her front porch swing, waiting for me.

She was crying out in the watches of the night, pouring out her heart for "the young ones that faint at the head of every street corner" (Lamentations 2:19). I could hear her prayers to God. It brings me to tears even now as I remember.

"God, help Bobby. He is like the young ones of Lamentations 2:19, that 'faint at the head of every street corner.'" Then she began to declare my destiny in God. "But, Bobby will be saved by you! He will be a compassionate warrior. He will touch many young people all over the world. He will help reform Christianity and bring new hope to many!"

She was a frail, eighty-five year old woman. She was not the pastor of a large church or a famous speaker. Many may have seen this woman as insignificant and her prayers as weak. But her prayers were more powerful than any ruler's decisions because she had a hope in her God and a special place before the King of Kings. Her prayers changed my life.

Aunt May was certain God heard and answered her prayers. There are many "Aunt May" pray-ers around the world whose hope in God moves mountains. Because of them the power of God is coming to the earth.

The Lord gave me a series of dreams that helped me understand the value He placed on those "Aunt Mays". He showed me the Houses Of Prayer arising around the earth filled with "the watchmen who cry out day and

HER PRAYERS WERE MORE POWERFUL THAN ANY RULER'S DECISION BECAUSE SHE HAD A HOPE IN HER GOD.

night" in hope (Isaiah 62:6 NIV), and explained that the prayers of these happy, hopeful intercessors would prepared the way for His kingdom to break in with new miracles, signs and wonders.

I know that no one is to personally take credit for God's move, but I saw in these dreams that the power of the faith-filled prayers of people like Aunt May was bringing the glory of God to the earth. Those who cry out night and day with hopeful expectation for their lives, their homes, their families, their churches and cities, will be rewarded with His appearing in those areas.

In these dreams, I also saw many leaders in the body of Christ, including some that I knew personally, who did not value the prayer of these Aunt Mays. The Lord rebuked them, exclaiming, "Leave her alone!" He cherishes the ministry of these Aunt Mays and expects the rest of us to seek Him the same way they do.

Aunt May hoped that her prayers would be heard and answered by God; she confidently expected that they would be and they were. She is a champion of hopeful prayer and her lifestyle is an invitation for us all to establish this pillar of hope in prayer.

HOPEFUL PRAYER

Prayer is the second pillar of hope because it unites our hearts to God who is the very essence of Hope. Prayer restores our hope as we connect to the power source of hope Himself, Jesus.

The Lord loves it when we draw near both for the sake of communion with Him and for the sake of advancing His kingdom. Daniel, Samuel, David, Solomon and so many others like, Samuel, Joshua, Abraham and Isaac, built kingdoms by staying on their knees. They knew it was necessary to meet with the God of hope through prayer in order to advance with strength.

"Aunt May" intercession builds a pillar of hope in our lives as we look to God to do the impossible. Like Terry, who sees more with her eyes closed than her eyes open we see with hopeful vision when we are untied to God in prayer. This place of prayer is the most glorious place from which to live and enables us to go forth in hope for every situation of life.

chapter six

PILLAR 3: HOPE IN PEOPLE

Be devoted to one another in love.
— Romans 12:10 NIV

LOOKING AT OTHERS WITH GOD'S EYES OF HOPE

Hope in God, and hope cultivated in prayer must lead to one place: hope in people. A few years before I encountered the Lord in the Chicago hotel room, I encountered the power of someone hoping in me because they carried the perspective of Jesus. This happened through my father.

When I left home as a teenager, I went from being a good student, my school's outstanding athlete and a leader among my peers to a fractured individual searching for meaning and validation.

My home had been a loving home, but after my mom became ill, pain ruled our home. My Dad was often absent because he had to work a number of jobs to pay my mom's medical bills. When he did come home, he was exhausted. I did not feel like there was anyone in my home who was available to teach me how to handle the challenges of life or to help meet my needs, so I left.

After the tragedy of the boy who drowned at the pool, I moved in with a roommate who was part of a notable band and together we started dealing cocaine. My older teenage years were a blur of drugs and partying. However, I still managed to finish high school; since my father was in education, he had helped me test out of certain courses and I had completed most of my high school education by my junior year before I left home. It was not difficult for me to complete school and I began a small business and became successful outwardly, but I was leading a dual life. I lived with no real sense of purpose in life or true hope for my future.

During these years, I had no relationship with my dad or my mom. I had divorced myself from the situation at home and cut myself off from my family. When I left home, I did not have any specific grudge against my parents, I was angry at everyone for not being there for me, but I was aware that many things were out of their control.

Dealing cocaine was a three-year nightmare. Everyday I hated what I had become. I lived in constant fear and dread of being arrested. One day, during a drug deal, a government informant was present. I was pretty sure he had identified me as a dealer. The government usually took several months to process the paperwork so I knew I had a few months to get out of town.

I registered for a General Psychology class at a community college a few towns away. I hoped that if I got away for a while they would lose my paperwork and I would be able to evade jail.

My roommate and I walked into the classroom and sat in the back. A few moments later the instructor walked into the room facing the chalkboard and began to write a rhetorical question on the board.

Immediately I recognized the teacher and the question he was writing. It was my father, and the question was a familiar exercise he had done with our family many times.

I interrupted him before he was able to finish writing on the board and answered the question he was about to lecture on. He put his piece of chalk down, turned towards the class, and said "Bobby?"

The registration list had only listed the class title, not the instructor's name. I had no idea he was to be my instructor. Obviously he had no idea I was in his class, either.

The class got quiet. "Bobby, your mom really misses you." I didn't have the heart to answer him. I just nodded. "Would you consider coming for Thanksgiving dinner in a few months?" he asked. Thanksgiving was the only time the whole family would be together and it was one of the few events my mom would save her energy to attend. I shook my head. I was not sure.

The room was stunned in silence and each person in the classroom could feel the weight of the interaction. After a few moments, Dad resumed teaching although he was still shaken. I darted out of the room as class was ending and did not give my Dad an opportunity to ask me any more questions.

For the next several weeks I skipped class most of the time. Class attendance was not required and I knew the material so I sent in homework with a friend. The night before Thanksgiving I remember making the decision to go see my family in order to honor my dad's request.

When my grandmother met me at the door, I wondered why I had come. My appearance screamed my hard-partying lifestyle, and my grandmother didn't like what she saw. "My, my you used to be a cute baby," she remarked, her tone a mix of sarcasm and sadness.

As I joined my family at the table, I was lost in feelings of my own worthlessness. I'd made such a mess out of my life. As I picked at the food on my plate, I became aware that someone was watching me. I looked up only to meet the eyes of my father. I'd been avoiding those eyes for months. When I met his eyes at the table, his eyes were filled with tears and full of affection for me.

He began to speak to me. "Bobby, you are going to be quite a man," he said. "You are going to touch a lot of lives." I couldn't receive these words of affirmation from him. I started to weep intensely with the weight of what I had become.

"Dad, do you know what I am?" I asked.

My issues were not a surprise to him. He said, "Son, I know who you are and I know you will pin your problems to the mat."

My dad hoped for a substantial life for me in my future. The young, foolish man sitting before him was still his pleasure and his dream. He valued me for who I was. Somehow he saw a different picture of my future. He saw past the depravity and called out the dignity of who I was. He expressed God's hopeful view of me with his words and actions.

MY DAD EXPRESSED GOD'S HOPEFUL VIEW OF ME WITH HIS WORDS AND ACTIONS.

I still went back to my lifestyle of sin and shame, all the while my father's words were ringing in my ear, "Son, you will be quite a man." I have never forgotten the vision of that gentle smile, those kind eyes, that hopeful perspective of my father. Though I didn't immediately repent of my lifestyle, my father's kind, gentle words marked me. God used them to help bring me to repentance a few years later in that Chicago hotel room.

SEEING PAST THE PAST

We have the opportunity to look past the negative, and see people with the eyes of Jesus. Those eyes see each one of us with hope and worth. Jesus proclaimed His mission statement, "The Spirit of the Lord is on me, because he has anointed me to preach good news to the poor. He has sent me to proclaim freedom for the prisoners and recovery of sight for the blind, to release the oppressed, to proclaim the year of the Lord's favor" (Luke 4:18,19 NIV). He states that His mission is to restore the beauty and worth of human beings. What a high value He has for us! It is why He came to the earth to live and die.

When we see ourselves and others through the eyes of disappointment and hopelessness, it is not the way Jesus sees us. That disappointment and hopelessness creates a dungeon of despair. When we allow ourselves to stay there, the enemy is able to build larger padlocks on the door so we become trapped in our own negative thinking towards others. We are at risk of living lives filled with meaningless relationships versus having hope-filled relationships like Jesus who loves and believes in each one of us.

Instead, we have a wondrous invitation to cultivate the seed of hope inside of ourselves towards others so that we can become fully alive and Jesus can free from us from the prisons of our own making.

God gifts us with His perspective of others if we are willing to pursue Him for it. I know in my life that God has given me a choice to have a "hurt view" of people where I remain hurt by their failures, or I can have a "love view" of people that sees them from God's perspective, like my father saw in me.

In the story of the prodigal son (Luke 15:11-32), the son returns home to the father to apologize for wasting his inheritance. He wants to see if he can rejoin his father's household, this time as a servant. The response of the father is stunning: "But while he was still a long way off, his father saw him and was filled with compassion for him; he ran to his son, threw his arms around him and kissed him" (Luke 15:20 NIV).

The fact that the father was even looking in the direction of the returning son tells us he was hopeful in his son that he would return. He had never given up hope on him.

The father ran to meet his son. For a landowner and man of prominence in that culture, running to meet his son was a completely undignified act. I believe he ran to meet his son not only because he was overjoyed to see him, but because he recognized his son was in despair and he could not stand to leave him there one moment longer. No cultural boundary would keep him from running to embrace his son in order to bring him back into the family and into a life of hope.

Such hope is in the heart of God for each person that is alive. Our God sees beyond our past failure, our present struggles and our future concerns. He views us as having an eternal position of value. Oh to see with His eyes for others and ourselves!

When you were around my dad, you could not believe anything but the best about yourself because that is what he believed. We all have the opportunity to extend our borders and become bigger and bigger in love, seeing past people's failures and lack. Then we will experience the transformative value of viewing others and ourselves with God's hope.

A FLOWER FOR ONE

Once we begin to see with the eyes of Jesus for others we realize the infinite worth of a single individual. Each person on earth is fearfully and wonderfully made (Psalm 139:14).

He has crowned us with glory and honor (Psalm 8:5). The knowledge of every good thing lies within each one for Christ's sake (Philemon 1:6). All around us, there are people without hope waiting for someone to offer them a message of hope and value.

Shortly after I was saved, I'd started a small business cleaning carpets and stripping floors in nursing homes. I went late one cold, rainy night to strip a floor at a nursing home on a rough side of town. I was fighting the flu, and was ready for the job to be finished before I'd even unloaded my van.

When I walked in the nursing home, I immediately heard loud cries for help from a woman in the nursing home, "Help me, help me, help me!" she was crying for someone to come care for her.

In that moment, I was reminded of the encounter I had had with the Lord in the stairwell shortly after I had been saved. I had seen several vivid scenes of people who had been devalued and needed hope. One of the five scenes was of an elderly woman, ignored and forgotten pushed up against a wall and crying out for someone to care for her and listen to her.

I felt the Lord's prompting to go talk to the woman who was crying out. I sat down in the hallway with my back against the wall, "God I am not man enough to help bring somebody out of such hopelessness into hope." After a while, I got myself up and headed her way.

When I entered her room, I saw her sitting in her wheelchair facing the wall, crying out for help. It was the exact woman I had seen in the encounter. I knew God had called me for this moment.

I turned her away from the wall and I started to straighten her dress. Her dress was rumpled and there was a blanket draped over her that was caught in her wheelchair. I began to try to untangle the blanket and arrange her things

HE HAS CROWNED US WITH GLORY AND HONOR.

PSALM 8:5

She shouted at me, thinking I was one of the caretakers, "Don't fix me! Stop looking after me! Would you please look at me?"

I stopped arranging her things and sat down on the edge of her bed, beside her wheelchair and turned towards her.

She said, "Don't look over my head. Look into my eyes. I have a story to tell if you would just listen."

I realized people were always doing things to her and for her, but never with her.

"Tell me your story," I said.

Over the next three weeks, I would head over to the nursing home at night and sit with her as she recounted her life's journey. Though she was probably in her eighties, she'd been neglected for years. I saw the power of hope expressed in her, however, as she came alive simply by having me ask her to tell me her story.

By making a little room for her in my heart and in my busy schedule, tremendous beauty and dignity came forth from her as she poured wisdom and life into me, possibly saving me from many years of mistakes through the valuable lessons she shared with me. She gave me golden insights and perspective about life. She taught me about relationships with my parents, how to treat women, to always be thankful, and to pray over things continually.

A transformation happened to her as she poured her life into me. I watched as she grew stronger and stronger as someone gave her the gift of their time and valued her life. It was not hard to do.

We each have the power to heal the sickness of hopelessness. This pillar of hope is built every time we choose to pay attention to the ones Jesus loves in our lives – which is every person! This story by Loren Eisley illustrates this principle perfectly:

> One day a man was walking along the beach when he noticed a boy picking something up and gently throwing it into the ocean. Approaching the boy, he asked, "What are you doing?"
>
> The youth replied, "Throwing starfish back into the ocean. The surf is up and the tide is going out. If I don't throw them back, they'll die."
>
> "Son," the man said, "don't you realize there are miles and miles of beach and hundreds of starfish? You can't make a difference!"

After listening politely, the boy bent down, picked up another starfish, and threw it back into the surf. Then, smiling at the man, he said... "I made a difference for that one."

Tell Them They Can Win

HAVING A HOPEFUL VIEW OF OTHERS INSPIRED THEM TO BE BETTER.

One afternoon at my college wrestling practice I saw the assistant coach pull the head coach aside to discuss another wrestler: "He's got a lot of heart, not a lot of talent for this level, but let's tell him he can win."

This guy had been very successful in high school but didn't stand a chance in competitions at the collegiate level.

"Even though his natural abilities don't reflect it, let's tell him he will be great!" The coach continued. So everyday they told him he was able to be a national competitor and that he was going to win.

To everyone's surprise he went on to take sixth place in the nation. At the end of the tournament he ran into the coach's arms in celebration. "You were right, coach! I really was that good!"

The coach smiled from ear to ear and said, "No, no you never really had that much talent. But you did have that much heart. We just told you that you were good because we knew how big of a heart you had and that you would rise up and believe it if we believed in you. You did it!"

The coach's belief in this wrestler helped me to understand what having a redemptive, hopeful view of others could do for them. It inspired them to be better than what their natural aptitudes or talents could accomplish in their lives. It often gifted them with an expanded ability and grace to be something beyond what they were or what they believed they were.

I also saw this principle with a young woman who is now my personal assistant. I was ministering to a large gathering of youth a few years ago and as I looked over the crowd, the Lord highlighted to me a young woman who I'd never met. As I looked at her I was tenderly touched by God's affection for her. She looked like a woman who was easily lost in a crowd and struggling to determine who she really was in God.

The Lord had showed me that she was functioning in life as "almost Amy", when her identity was really "amazing Amy". I called her out during the service and the Lord impacted her deeply in hope. As a result of expressing God's hopeful view of her identity, she has blossomed in life.

A few months after that initial meeting, I ended up hiring her as my personal assistant. Over the last few years, I have seen a major transformation happen in her life. She used to think little of herself and her capacities but now she is someone who manages a very large amount of responsibility with ease. She oversees people and projects with excellence, always with a smile of hope on her face. She constantly speaks with an understanding of God's hope in people and is always unlocking the treasure in others. She truly is "amazing Amy!"

Hoping in people is recognizing and releasing the resources of God in them. Hope opens people up to who they are versus who they are not. It helps them to look at themselves with appreciation versus critical analysis. It launches them into their God-ordained destinies!

There are a thousand voices constantly telling people what they are not. We can take a stand for who they really are in God. It's time to believe in people even beyond their capacities! We can watch people rise up to possibilities beyond their own assessment of themselves as we call forth the gold in them.

LOVE BECOMES EASY

Like my father did for me on Thanksgiving so many years ago, we each have the opportunity to look past the current condition of a person to their eternal identity in God. Then speaking their identity and destiny according to a hopeful view is one of the most powerful tools we have to establish hope inside of hearts. We can do this both for others and for ourselves as we continue on this journey of hope.

chapter seven

PILLAR 4: HOPE IN THE NEXT GENERATION

The future belongs to those who
give the next generation reason to hope.
— Pierre Teilhard de Chardin

SEEING THE BEAUTY OF THE NEXT GENERATION

In the late eighties, I was a youth pastor for Kansas City Fellowship and had the privilege of working periodically with John Wimber, leader of the Vineyard movement. John had an incredible reach across the nations and a tremendous impact on generations. One afternoon when I was at a gathering with him in San Louis Obispo, California, I had the chance to dialogue with him about the next generation.

"How are the youth you are overseeing in Kansas City doing?" he asked.

I began to complain. "They're all against me. I'm going to write a book comparing them to communist infiltrators who want to destroy my life."

It was a weak attempt at humor, but it was obvious to John that I was speaking out of true disappointment. My disappointment came out of my own weariness at the difficulty of doing youth ministry. In those days, I would consider it a successful meeting if no one died or became pregnant during a youth gathering. I was beyond fed up with their spiritual apathy. I didn't yet have a true hope in God for the next generation.

John was gazing out the window at something I could not see. There was a long silence before he turned to face me. "Bob, they're beautiful," he whispered.

His response shook me. It started to touch the very core of my hurt and disappointment and I began to see the youth with the perspective of a patriarch. The next generation is not a distraction or a problem, and they are not to be labeled Generation 'X', 'Y', or 'Z'". They are to be called "Generation HOPE!"

When Terry and I were in Israel many years ago, I had an opportunity to listen to an animated conversation among several older men sitting on a park bench who were watching some children playing. These patriarchs discussed one preschool boy in great detail, speculating about what kind of person he would become when he grew up. Each one took such ownership of his success that I was not able to tell which man was the boy's father; they all saw him as beautiful and had such hope for his future.

This patriarchal view of the next generation, like John Wimber and those Israeli patriarchs carried, is so invaluable! It is coming into agreement with the Lord's hopeful perspective of them, calling them forth into the destiny the Lord has planned for them, beyond all that we could ask or think!

While the pillar of Hope In People is hope in God in the nature of a human being created in His image, the pillar of Hope In The Next Generation is a hope in the future. It is the confidence that God is able on a whole other level to bring forth victory with our littlest and weakest weapons... the children.

FIGHTING FOR THEIR FUTURE

My approach to ministry to the next generation was dynamically transformed when I realized I was to fight for the next generation instead of fighting against them.

Through my life, most of my athletic coaches had trained me to succeed out of determination, anger, and frustration. Within a few months of my salvation, I was placed in a position of leadership with the ministry of Fellowship of Christian Athletes and I bean to apply the same methods that my coached had taught me. For years I led several hundred youth and young adults through FCA and through church youth groups. My leadership style was to try to kick them into shape because I believed that they were not good enough. In my mind, they were rebellious children and they needed to be reminded of that fact continually. I tried to control them and dominate them.

I REALIZED I WAS TO FIGHT FOR THE NEXT GENERATION.

This type of leadership style was not one of love. I found that when the young ones failed or found themselves in sin, they would not come to me. They did not feel like they could open up their hearts and lives to me, because they felt I would be angry and disappointed, and at that stage, I would have been. As a result, many of them would go deeper into the sin or the problem, as they didn't think I would accept or receive them in their failures. Because they received this view of leadership from me, many had the same perception of God the Father. Many believed that He was disappointed and angry, and missed the truth that the Father was longing with open arms for them to run to Him, not from Him, as we see in the parable of the prodigal son and his father in Luke 15.

My lack of love in leadership was made clear to me one night at a conference where I had been invited to speak on the subject of love. The man who was introducing me was extolling all of my qualifications to speak on the subject of love. As I was walking up to the stage after the lofty introduction, a woman came out of the row where she had been sitting and intercepted me as I walked to the podium. She shouted to me in front of the crowd, "You are the last one qualified to speak on love!" I was stung. I did not know how to respond.

She went on to say that I had damaged her daughter who was a part of my youth group. The young lady had become pregnant, and because of my lack of love and my judgmental spirit, she did not feel she was able to come to me for help. Later, she ran away from home, feeling she had no one to support her. Her mother blamed me for the tragedy, and it broke my heart.

As I continued the seemingly long walk up to the stage to preach on love, the Lord began to speak to me. He asked me, "Are you going to believe the truth of this accusation, or the greater truth of who I have called you to be in love?"

I made a decision to move forward in the Father's love and forgiveness, despite my weaknesses. I could have rightfully disqualified myself as one unworthy to speak on the subject of love, but the Lord gave me a challenge.

Either I could believe in my perceived condition as a broken sinner, or I could believe in my position as a lover of God and of people despite my weaknesses. I chose the latter, and I preached my heart out as if I did not hear the enemy's accusations regarding my unworthiness. Yes, the enemy was speaking truth. I was unworthy, but the Lord helped me to hold fast to a greater truth. The Father's hope in me and unconditional love for me is more than enough to compensate for my weaknesses! My position is secure, not because of my perfect commitment to Him, but His commitment in me. So I apologized to the mother from the depths of my heart and then shared the greatest message on love that I think I had ever shared.

Immediately, I began to grow in confidence of my position as a lover of people and a patriarch versus my present condition of filtering people through a lens of disappointment. I began to see the next generation through the lenses of hope, that they too, were greatly loved by the Father, and His love and ability to overcome their weaknesses was so much greater than any challenge and sin they faced. With an impartation of the hopeful perspective of John Wimber and others, I was able to believe God is able to redeem young people and build them. I started to see the reality of God's greatness in the youth. I saw the value of mentoring and began let go of my constant concern that they were going to disappoint me.

The Lord is offered me a whole new approach to draw out young ones and speak with the hope of God over their lives. Terry and I made a decision early on in our family that we would never be referees for petty fights among our children; we were going to be proactive about speaking to our children the hope of who they will be in God.

For example, in raising any child, there are always chal-lenges, but one day I felt like the Lord spoke to me regarding our son, Jedidiah. The Lord said joyously to me, "You will never have a problem with him. Enjoy him." And that is how we have purposed to raise him. This exhortation from the Lord has shifted my perspective of my son ever since. Now I focus on seeing him for the treasure that he is and the promises God has for him instead of assuming that it is my role to act as a prison warden over his life.

VIEWING YOUNG PEOPLE AS A BLESSING
AND NOT A HINDRANCE

The disciples viewed the young ones as a hindrance in Matthew 18, but Jesus had a different perspective. "The little children were brought to Jesus for him to place his hands on them and pray for them. But the disciples rebuked those who brought them. Jesus said, "Let the little children come to me, and do not hinder them, for the kingdom of heaven belongs to such as these" (Matthew 19:14 NIV). Jesus invited them in to be with Him and even said that the kingdom of heaven belongs to them and those like them! He took it a step further when He said we must become like children to enter His kingdom!

God has given me an invitation to move from attitude of the disciples to the perspective of Jesus. Like the disciples, we can see young people as a hindrance to our ministry and an inconvenience. But Jesus opened His heart to them and welcomed them.

I long to be proactive in loving the next generation. When I am challenged with having a hopeful perspective of the next generation, I like to ask God questions about them according to His perspective. "How have you assured his or her success in you, Lord?", "What is the treasure that lies inside of him?", "Tell me what you like about this group of young men and women, Father." This helps me to stop looking at them with critical analysis according to the flesh and helps me to see them from God's perspective.

I LONG TO BE PROACTIVE IN LOVING THE NEXT GENERATION.

Sometimes it is hard work to develop love and appreciation for young people. We call it discernment when we are "wise" enough to see one another's weaknesses, but according to God, this is foolishness. It is easy to see the challenge at hand, but it sometimes it takes a second look to see the beauty within young people and to call it forth. When the decision is made to call forth their beauty and destiny in the Lord, eternal fruit is produced and lives are transformed!

I witnessed a powerful example of this reality as I observed my dad and his interactions with a young lady named Loretta. My dad was overseeing an inner-city school at the time, and Loretta was a sixth grade student who would physically challenge the other children and misbehave in class. The teachers would constantly report to my dad about Loretta's unruly behavior. My dad tried reaching her, but nothing seemed to work. Finally, he had a brilliant idea. In order to call forth the very best in Loretta, he decided the teaching staff needed to let her know that they believed in her and that she was valued and loved as a gift to them.

Dad brought Loretta into his office the next day. Although she could barely read, he asked her to teach the first graders the alphabet. He called out the leadership potential in her. Dad reached from his desk and pulled out a golden nametag. It read "Loretta," with the word "Teacher" on the bottom.

Loretta rose up to every bit of Dad's hope for her. She soared as she taught the younger ones, and oh how they loved her! Years later, she ended up becoming a teacher. That experience taught me an invaluable lesson. I learned that even the most difficult child has so much potential when they are believed in and loved for who they are, and not constantly reminded of what they are not. When a child's heart is unlocked so he understands his value, destiny and calling in the Lord, hope can lift them up beyond our wildest expectations.

Children are a reward and a blessing. "Behold, children are a heritage from the Lord, the fruit of the womb a reward" (Psalm 127:3). They are our inheritance. They are precious to God's heart and key to the advancement of His kingdom.

"I love the devotion of your youth" (Jeremiah 2:2 NIV). David prayed, "Oh that our daughters will be like pillars and palaces; that our sons will be fully alive plants" (Psalm 144:12 NIRV). The Father has such dreams in His heart for each one of them! When we see those dreams and believe in them, partnering with the Lord's heart for them, young people can rise up to every bit of their potential in God.

HELP THEM DRAW NEAR

Children can be fearful of entrance into God's presence if they perceive themselves incorrectly. When they are believed in, they are confident before God and confident in all of life. They are able to see the God who really does want to encounter them and they no longer fear being accepted by Him.

WHEN WE TELL YOUNG PEOPLE WHO THEY ARE, THEY SEE THE PLANS GOD HAS FOR THEM.

When we tell young people who they are, they see the plans for their future and welfare that He has for them. He has such success planned for each one. We must help them to believe it!

My daughter Taylor has never had an identity problem. She has always seen herself as wonderful. She will even kiss herself. One day I saw her looking in the mirror and I asked her, "Taylor what do you see?"

"Only good things," she said with a smile. I agreed.

She has been told consistently that she is beautiful, that God loves her and that she will succeed. This way, she is never afraid of life or afraid to come before God boldly and assuredly. She is confident in her identity!

But my youngest daughter, Bethany, needed a little more help discovering her true worth. One time I saw her looking in the mirror and I asked her the same question: "What do you see, Bethany?"

She said, "I see ugly".

I set her up on the counter and held her face and said, "No, this is who Bethany is. She is beautiful. She is God's delight. She is one of the most compassionate young ladies I know. She cares about her friends, she will cry when they cry, laugh when they laugh. Bethany is bountiful in life, abundant in joy. Bethany is daring, she will run after trials and she will succeed. Bethany is a wondrous young lady with heart and life. Bethany moves God's heart and He loves her tremendously." Her countenance changed as she began to believe who she was. She just needed to be reminded.

I constantly tell each one of my four children, "Go for it! You are attacking life, you are succeeding". God wants them not only to survive, but thrive in this life. My son and daughters are experiencing the blessings of abundant life because others have expressed hope in and for them. They are confident in all arenas of life: education, work, relationships, and ministry. They know who they are and are confident in their lives and walk with God!

Establish Their Identity

My heart's desire is that we would become patriarchs and matriarchs for young people, telling them that they are more than conquerors, they are mighty ones. We have an invitation to do what Jesus did for John, telling him he was not an angry son of thunder, but an apostle of love, the beloved. He called him forth into his place of true worth. He did the same for Peter. Though his name meant "a small stone", Jesus believed in him and called him a rock.

Once we speak to a young person their true identity in Him, they can believe it themselves. All it takes is for a father, a brother, or a friend to come along and speak identity and worth to them. My father did this for me many times through my youth and it anchored a greater hope inside of me. His interaction with me has been an example to me of how to hope in the next generation.

In my elementary school, we had an annual students versus teachers softball game. It was the biggest event of the year. Throughout the history of the school, the students had never won. This year was going to be different. I was pitching and the game was going surprisingly well.

I sensed that I was about to single-handedly rewrite the story of these games. I'd hit two home runs, and if we could prevent the teachers from scoring, we'd win the game. I envisioned the celebration that was about to happen in my honor: women were screaming my name, children were crying my praises, newspaper reporters were taking my picture. Victory was in my grasp!

In the last inning of the game with a teacher on third, I pitched the ball to the batter. To my delight, she hit it straight to me. I quickly grabbed it and threw it as hard as I could. I should have thrown it to first base or home for an easy out, but for some reason beyond my understanding, I threw it to second base. The ball rolled past the second baseman into the center field and the teachers ran home scoring the winning runs. I quickly went from the "Great One" to the "Goat". I was so devastated.

On the way home, about ten of my buddies were hiding in the woods ready to beat me up. I took the long way home to avoid an untimely death.

When I arrived home, my dad asked me to go for a walk. He assured me that everything would be okay. He told me people would forget my failure and talked to me about all the potential I carried for my future, outside of softball.

Young people so easily perceive their little mistakes as huge failures. I thought my world had ended. But my dad offered me hope for my future; he put the situation back in context by convincing me that one silly little softball game did not define my whole future.

I went back to school on Monday morning with a plan. Before the morning announcements, I sneaked into the administration office and began speaking on the school intercom, "This is 'Forgive Bob Hartley Day'. Bob Hartley will not be defined by one forty-five minute event. Bob Hartley has a great future. One day, he will do wonderful things. He will run hotdog stands and become a professional wrestler."

Hearing the footsteps of some of the teachers pounding down the hallway, I quickly ended with, "So hug him when you see him!" and I ran off.

My dad had successfully imparted his vision of a hopeful future for me, and I was able to confidently proclaim it. In fact, I proved to be so entertaining on the intercom that I was asked to do morning announcements each day. (Until I declared a co-ed wrestling match between two teachers who liked each other, thus ending my career.)

Sowing Hope Brings Healing To The Generations

I have discovered that when you sow life, hope and appreciation into the next generation, you tend to reap it as well. I saw this happen on Christmas with my father who had continually sown a message of God's hope into our lives.

When I was a child, the kids in my family would give my father gag gifts for Christmas. We would take turns presenting silly poems or witty criticism to him. My siblings were all very bright and could be quite entertaining. My dad always played along with this tradition in good fun.

One year, however, the routine changed. My oldest sister began to read her poem, but for some reason she couldn't continue. She crumpled the paper she held in her hand, threw it to the floor and looked my dad in the eyes. "Dad, I have never met a man like you. You are as gentle a man I have ever known. You are so honorable and kind."

My brother picked up where she left off. "Yeah, Dad. You never get worried and burdened, you always turn hard things into joyful things."

Another sister shared, "When I get married, Dad, I want to marry a man like you."

The next brother began, "Dad, you are unpretentious, you never pretend. You are so sincere and I want to grow up to be a man like you."

I tucked myself behind the Christmas tree and cried. I loved to see my father loved, hoped in, believed in, and appreciated, as he had done for us countless times! It moved me deeply to see my father cared for and valued in this way. Now that I am a father, nothing moves me like my children caring for my heart and loving me in return!

JOINING THE GENERATIONS

The Bible says that God "will restore the hearts of the fathers to their children and the hearts of the children to their fathers, so that I will not come and smite the land with a curse" (Malachi 4:6).

These words go far beyond wishful thinking. They are the key to transforming relationships, generations and nations. Through the power of the Holy Spirit we can communicate hope in a way that His message is comprehended by the next generation. This will turn the hearts of the father towards the children, and the hearts of the children to the Father. When that happens, our land will be blessed.

WHEN WE TREAT YOUNG PEOPLE AS A BLESSING WE WILL HAVE A HEALING IN OUR NATION.

When we treat young people as a blessing we will have a healing in our nation. The children we delivered will deliver us. They will become sons and daughters "of the right hand", the position of honor, that will uphold us in the times to come. But before this happens, we must first believe in them and impart God's true, hopeful view of them.

HOPEFUL VIEW

Jesus led the way in blessing and accepting the next generation. I have learned through people like my dad and John Wimber, as well as countless others, that the next generation is to be fought for, not fought against. What an opportunity we have to hope in them even when we do not see potential for good! We get to look with the eyes of God and have an eternal perspective for the next generation. And what a blessing we will receive when the generations are partnered together in hope. Let's go on this journey of seeing the next generation with the hopeful eyes of God.

chapter eight

PILLAR 5: HOPE IN CITIES AND NATIONS

In His name, the nations will put their hope.
— Matthew 12:21 NIV

THE 1983 VISION OF THE CITY

The last pillar of hope is Hope In Cities And Nations. God's hope is bigger than just the four walls of the church and the people that dwell inside of them. His hope reaches to every inch of the earth. He loves cities and nations, the earth is His creation and the people in it are His desired dwelling place.

His heart is fixed on specific geographic areas and the life that dwells in them. He has hope for every arena of life within the cities and nations of the earth, including government, business and education. He is the author of it all! Hebrews 3:4 says that "...the builder of all things is God."

In 1983, I was overcome with a longing to understand what the Lord was feeling and what He cared about. I asked

Him over and over, "Father, what is on Your heart? What are Your heart's desires?" The Lord answered my prayer in an open vision in a stairwell in Fort Collins. I received from the Lord "the Vision of the City" that helped me understand the weightiness of God's desire for cities and nations and His hope for what they can become. This vision captured my heart and I have never been the same.

In the vision, I was sitting on a hill overlooking a large city. From this vantage point, I watched as Jesus walked through the streets of the city. My heart broke as I saw that no one noticed Him. As He walked through, He was not perceived by the inhabitants of the city, and was not being loved or valued by them. I could sense that the people's hearts were far from Him.

Their confidence in Him had waned and they were living under the clouds of discouragement. I sensed that the people of this city had lost their hopeful view a long time ago. A "theology of barrenness and hopelessness" had come in where the prevailing thought said that God was not near to them in their jobs, families, activities and even in their churches.

As I watched this, I could sense a longing in the Father heart of God for the entire city to dance a dance of love for

His Son. He desired to the see city respond to His Son and be filled with confident hope in Him. Oh how He longed for them!

Then, the scene shifted. Supernaturally, the city was transformed into the place it was meant to be in God according to His dream for it. I saw Jeremiah 33:9 (NIV) written over the city: "Then this city will bring me renown, joy, praise and honor before all nations on earth that hear of all the good things I do for it; and they will be in awe and will tremble at the abundant prosperity and peace I provide for it".

God's banner over this city was His joy and His hope! I saw the city's inhabitants begin to recognize the form and moving of God in their circumstances and their cities. Their courage and hope was restored in Him.

It became a city that understood that He is the God of all of life and celebrated Him in every arena of practical life including government, education, family and church.

"Pioneers of practical intimacy" filled the city. These were ones who loved to discover God's presence in all arenas of life. As a result, the people were unified in their cry of response: "Give us intimacy with You in every area of our lives or give us death!"

In the vision, I saw eighty people who were called to "sing a song of wisdom," over cities and nations all over the earth. These eighty people were called to unlock God's wise plans for entire geographic regions. Twenty years later, I have met almost all of the faces I saw in that vision.

As I looked over the transformed city, I was reminded of the Deuteronomy 6 commandment to tell our children how good He is and of His promises, because it says in verse 10 that we will receive "flourishing cities you did not build" (Deuteronomy 6:10 NIV). This was such a splendid city.

GOD WANTED ME TO PERCEIVE CITIES AND NATIONS THROUGH THE EYES OF GOD'S DESIRE FOR THEM.

This vision showed me what this verse could look like. I understood that God wanted me to perceive cities and nations through the eyes of God's desire for them. I wasn't supposed to respond to the condition of these geographical places in the present, but according to what God longed for them to become: places of hope, places that recognized the beauty of His Son.

I began to spend hours each day walking and talking with Him about cities and nations. As I did, hope grew in me to see whole cities and nations celebrating His presence and loving Him well.

I dreamed that stadiums in America, and also across the world, were filled with thousands and thousands of people worshiping the Lord and declaring that Jesus is loved within their cities. The scoreboards in the stadiums read, "Jesus is loved well here".

I dreamed that Wall Street would one day become Worship Street and that our banks would become bountiful in benevolence. They'd be places where the generosity of God is upheld versus operating out of a "spirit of fear and greed." I dreamed that the education system would glorify God as the Creative One, full of ingenuity and genius.

Sometimes it feels as if I dreamed an impossible dream as I watch cities and nations slide into greater and greater ungodliness. At times, my hope has waned. During one of these times of discouragement, I had another dream in which the Lord challenged me.

"You don't believe cities and nations can change do you? You yourself were so far backslidden, so far away Me. Yet you changed through a little bit of my love. Why can't you believe for cities and nations that I have called?" He asked. "Why don't you tell Nineveh it doesn't work to believe in Me? Why don't you tell the whole region of Samaria, viewed as unclean by her Jewish neighbors, that they cannot ever be clean and holy in Me? Why don't you tell Antioch and Ephesus, the Hebrides Islands, tell Macedonia, tell Wales. Tell them my power to transform cannot come and change a city or a nation." His loving rebuke showed me I was in danger of losing His hope for the cities and nations the Lord has chosen for Himself.

I have never lost that picture of the hopeful city. I have meditated deeply into this vision a million times. Before I die, I long to see many cities and nations whose hope is God, as I saw in that vision in 1983.

Saint Catherine's Gardens

Since 1983, I have begun to see cities and nations come forth into a destiny of hope. I have participated in bringing the message of God's love and hope to nations like Australia, Norway, New Zealand, South Korea, Zimbabwe, as well as many other places. God is bringing this message of hope to cities and nations all over the world. It has been my joy to participate in sharing God's promises over some of these cities and nations.

The Lord gave me a pattern of what even a little bit of hope can look like when I remember the experience I had in my childhood neighborhood called St. Catherine's Garden, in southern Kansas City.

St. Catherine's Garden was kid heaven. There were hundreds of kids in the neighborhood because most of the families had five to fifteen children. The Thomas family across the street had eight; the Earls had seven, the Johnsons down the way had sixteen! Our summers and evenings were spent playing in the streets; shouting and laughter could be heard on every block.

Each family cared for one another's children as if they were their own. I remember taking baths with Joe Thomas and stealing cookies from the Thomas's cupboards. Many nights, I would sneak over to their home for a midnight snack. I experienced the best this neighborhood had to offer a boy: a safe, welcoming place where a community truly shared life together.

As a young boy, I would walk on the sidewalks and dream great things for this neighborhood that I loved so much. I prayed that children all over the world could experience what I experienced in this place. In my little-boy ramblings, I also asked God to establish St. Catherine's as a neighborhood that would worship Him forever and go forth to touch the world with hope.

Now, forty years later, St. Catherine's Gardens is where the International House of Prayer in Kansas City has been planted. The neighborhood has now become a place where thousands of people come to join a movement of night and day prayer and worship. I have been able to witness this powerful move of God coming forth from my old neighborhood.

The Lord answered my prayer of hope for my neighborhood. It is not a completely, instantly transformed place, but amazing things are happening there and hope is coming forth. God is so faithful to answer our cries for cities and nations!

NEW FREEDOMS FOR NATIONS

We have a dear family friend, Bob Jones, who is a prophetic voice to the nations. In 2008, both Bob Jones and I each heard the Lord speak regarding fifty nations across the earth that would be dedicated to the Lord. Bob Jones gave us the example of Fiji, a nation that was dedicated to the Lord on a national level in one day in the year 2001.

The Lord showed us that there would be many other nations like Fiji. This movement would begin in Norway, then travel to the U.S. and fifty other nations around the world. He desires to give these nations a "name of honor" according to His hopeful view of them.

The Lord is giving an invitation to us to appeal to His heart to change the course of history according to His view of hope for cities and nations. "If my people, who are called by my name, will humble themselves and pray and seek my face and turn from their wicked ways, then will I hear from heaven and will forgive their sin and will heal their land" (II Chronicles 7:14 NIV). If we gather together to repent and seek His face, there will be great healing in our land.

There is power in cooperate gatherings because there is an unlocking of love that cannot not be unlocked by a single individual. I believe that if we repent and seek His face, God will establish our homes, businesses and organizations as "hope centers" – places where prayer and worship are their foundation, and their members communicate confident expectation in God in all their interactions.

Hopeful prayer is our weapon as we fight for cities and nations. In this season, the devil may be releasing his weapons, but God is releasing His arsenal as well. God's arsenal is a spirit of hopeful worship and intercession that will arise from people who long to see God establish victorious and hope-filled cities and nations.

As the enemy unleashes his weapons, we can remember God's goodness and magnify the Lord's unrelenting kindness in the past and the present. A heritage of hope will spring forth in those cities and nations that invite the God of hope to be their Lord.

THE STORY OF SOWETO

Terry and I visited South Africa during the waning days of apartheid. The legislated racial discrimination caused great national turmoil. At the time we were there, the country was one of the most violent places on earth.

During our stay, Terry and I visited a home group of believers that worshiped together in a shanty in Soweto. Most people in the country were held in bondage to the frustration of the social, economic and spiritual effects of apartheid, but this small group showed us the power of hope expressed in love and forgiveness.

There was a gracious, kind woman leading the gathering. When the meeting began, she surprised Terry and I with the roar that came forth from her soul as she prayed and worshiped. This woman was unmovable in her hope in God. Her hope in people was evident as well, as she was leading and celebrating the others. That evening she was praying for and blessing a man standing next to her.

A HERITAGE OF HOPE WILL SPRING FORTH IN THOSE CITIES AND NATIONS THAT INVITE THE GOD OF HOPE TO BE THEIR LORD.

I whispered to someone beside me, "Who is that man she is blessing?" The person replied that this was the man who had killed her brother while she was forced to watch. After the murder, she pursued him with a love that was greater than her offense. He received the Lord and became her right-hand man. That night, she was prophesying over him, expressing God's hope about who this man was meant to be before Him.

This little group brought transformation to those they touched as a result of their hope. They impacted their whole city with this force of hope. Many of the leaders in the city and country were reported that they visited this city because of the hope coming forth from it. They were a hope center for their whole city even in the midst of the incredibly difficult circumstances! When the darkness is so great, we have the greatest opportunity to shine as a hope center for whole cities and nations.

Hope For Cities And Nations

With the "Vision of The City" that the Lord gave me years ago, I have learned to begin to view cities according to God's hopeful view and according to His desires. We are invited to take our place in God's kingdom to intercede for the nations. He desires the earth to be His resting place.

It will take a strong decision to have a whole new perspective and attack the doubts and the cynicism of the past in a radical way. We can pray that whole cities will make this decision and it will lead to wholesale change, and a new and deeper understanding of hope in God.

Places like the shanty in Soweto will come forth with hope and love that are beacons for their cities and God will restores His purposes in the cities and nations as hope centers are established. God will be extolled in all arenas of life in the midst of the cities and nations of the earth.

section three

❧

An Invitation
To Go On
The Journey
Of Hope

chapter nine
JESUS, THE MAN OF HOPE

Truly Jesus is the center of our hope.

JESUS' JOURNEY OF TRUE HOPE

My life long quest for hope has led me to one Man. He is the embodiment of the five pillars of hope and of this hope journey. Jesus Himself is the foundation and cornerstone of a hope-filled life. Jesus is a reflection of His Father, who is a God filled with hope. He is not severe and distant but is full of love.

As I have sought to establish the five pillars of hope in my life, the Lord has instructed me to examine the life of Jesus according to hope. I can now see the Jesus who is the Man of Hope and the One who is a perfect revelation of His Father. The journey of hope that Jesus led while He was on the earth is worthy of study, worthy of appreciation, and worthy of pursuit as we begin our own journeys of hope. He is the perfect demonstration of hope in the five pillars and in all arenas of life.

I could spend years simply unfolding the revelation of the beauty of the Man of hope, the Lord Jesus; His Father, the God of hope; and the Holy Spirit. One day I hope to write more on this, but for now here is a taste of some of the ways Jesus has led me on this journey of hope.

HOPE IN GOD

The most beautiful relationship that has ever existed is the one between our heavenly Father, the Holy Spirit, and Jesus, the Son. The perfect unity, trust and love between the members of the Trinity surpasses human comprehension (Ephesians 3:19). The way Jesus hoped in His Father gives us a perfect picture to follow as we learn to hope in God in our lives. He demonstrated perfect relationship with the Father.

The richness of the beauty of God is displayed in the hope the Son had in His Father while He walked the earth. Jesus said, "I and the Father are one" (John 10:30 NIV). He did not move, act or speak outside of the Father's will. Jesus' hope in His Father was not characterized by slave-like drudgery, but by the delight He took in doing His Father's will.

Jesus showed immense hope in His Father by choosing to even come to the earth. He made Himself of no reputation, vulnerable and weak (Philippians 2:7). He submitted to His Father, laid aside all His rights as God, and became a human being. He trusted the Father to guide and protect Him through every season of His life, death and resurrection on earth.

We can see Jesus' confidence in His relationship with His Father during His growing-up years. He headed to the temple in Jerusalem (Luke 2:46,47) to speak about His Father with the educated religious people there. This was the act of a Man confident in His Father's character and love.

At the inauguration of His ministry, Jesus was baptized as an act of obedience to His Father. The Holy Spirit was present that day in the form of a dove. The Trinity manifested itself

THE RICHNESS OF THE BEAUTY OF GOD IS DISPLAYED IN THE HOPE THE SON HAD WITH HIS FATHER.

in Voice, dove and Son, blessing Christ's obedience (Matthew 3:13-17), and the Spirit led Him immediately into the desert for forty days of testing. Jesus expressed unwavering hope in God at the end of that time. He proclaims that He will hope in God alone and live from every word that proceeds from His Father's mouth: "Man shall not live by bread alone, but by every word that proceeds from the mouth of God" (Matthew 4:4).

Throughout Jesus' entire ministry on earth, He hoped in His Father's direction, obedient to everything the Father led Him to do. As He ministered to the multitudes and healed the masses (Matthew 15:30), the Father was His sole source of strength.

At the end of Jesus' earthly life, when He faced the terrifying course of crucifixion, He said to His Father, "Please take this cup from me, but not my will but yours be done" (Luke 22:42 NIV). He expressed hope in His Father with both words and the ultimate obedient action – His death, when His Father turned His face from Him. The reward for this agony was His resurrection and the salvation of His bride!

Jesus knew the limitless greatness of His Father, and He chose to put His entire trust in Him. Jesus loved the

Father with all His heart. The Son honored His Father in every way.

This same hope Jesus had was a demonstration of the Father's hope. Jesus shared the story of the Prodigal Son to show us the kind of hope the Father has for each one of us. Jesus tells the story of a returning son and the love and joy a father has at his return (Luke 15:11-31). The father in the parable hoped in the lost son's return, persisted in his prayers for his son, and waited expectantly for his son to come home. When the son returned, the father was the first to greet him with an explosion of love and celebration. What a picture of a loving, hopeful father!

Jesus demonstrated the Hope of God and His hope in God with every move He made on earth. He revealed the Hope of His Father. We are His bride, and He has given us an inheritance of hope.

Hope In Prayer

Jesus manifested His hope in God through His obedience and confidence in God, and through a living connection with Him. Jesus demonstrated His life of hope in God by living a life of prayer.

"After he had dismissed them, he went up on a mountainside by himself to pray. When evening came, he was there alone" (Matthew 14:23 NIV). Scripture contains a number of accounts of Jesus hiding away in order to pray; He loved to talk to His Father. He treasured these times of prayer. They offered Him time to be refreshed in His Father's presence so that He could bring revelation and miracles to cities.

WE HOPE IN GOD BY LIVING A LIFE OF PRAYER.

Jesus instructed His disciples to pray (Luke 11:2-4). He knew the importance of establishing a connection with God through prayer and wanted to ensure that those who followed Him would have the same.

Prayer is referenced over sixty times in the gospels, Jesus was recorded praying or He was teaching His disciples to pray.

John 13-17 contains not only Jesus' teachings about His relationship with His Father and us, and our relationships with one another, but also His prayer for His bride. He left a rich deposit of prayer to God for the welfare of His followers before He ascended to the right hand of the Father.

"Christ Jesus, who died--more than that, who was raised to life--is at the right hand of God and is also interceding for us" (Romans 8:34 NIV). Even now, He is in heaven interceding on our behalf. Not only did Jesus hope in prayer while He was on the earth, but Jesus prays eternally!

HOPE IN PEOPLE

I find myself continually amazed by the way Jesus hoped in people. He was never disappointed by a repentant heart, and never rejected anyone. He views people with eternal love, seeing past their current condition and calls them into their destiny as a member of His spotless bride.

Even a brief skim through the gospels will show you the way Jesus expressed hope in broken people. Jesus told the truth to the woman He met at the well about her adulterous history in her marriages (John 4), but the forgiveness and hope He expressed to her transformed her into an evangelist to a whole city. Jesus shared a meal with the crooked businessman and thief Zacchaeus . His hope in Zacchaeus is shown by Jesus' eagerness to spend time with him in fellowship (Luke 19:5). Zacchaeus was forever changed by that one encounter with Jesus. Jesus saved the life of the woman caught in adultery with a single sentence (John 8:11) then expressed hope in her by telling her to go and to sin no more.

Jesus expressed hope in His disciples, even though Peter would deny Him and Judas would betray Him. The others all had moments of unbelief, doubt, pride and ambition. And yet, when He ascended into heaven after His resurrection, He entrusted them to carry the news about Him to the ends of the earth!

What's extraordinary about this hope is contained in Jesus' mercy-filled whisper from the cross: "Father, forgive them; for they know not what they do" (Luke 23:34 KJV). His sacrifice is the ultimate expression of hope to be reconciled with each one of us who'd been alienated from the Father by our sin.

HOPE IN THE NEXT GENERATION

Jesus loved children and young people! "People were also bringing babies to Jesus to have him touch them. When the disciples saw this, they rebuked them. But Jesus called the children to him and said, 'Let the little children come to me, and do not hinder them, for the kingdom of God belongs to such as these'" (Luke 18:16 NIV). He wanted to bless the next generation with a touch of hope!

In addition to welcoming children, Jesus asked His adult followers to become like them. "Truly, I say to you, unless you turn and become like children, you will never enter the kingdom of heaven. Whoever humbles himself like this child is the greatest in the kingdom of heaven" (Matthew 18:3-4).

Jesus Himself came as a child, the government of heaven resting upon His shoulders. He commands us to receive the next generation for when we do, we receive Him. "Whoever receives one such child in my name receives me" (Mark 9:37).

Scripture is full of accounts of Jesus healing children and even raising them from the dead (Mark 19:14-29, Mark 5:35-41, Luke 7:11-17). He has hope for the future of the next generation and will not stand back and allow the enemy to steal their futures, vitality, health and lives!

HOPE IN CITIES AND NATIONS

The gospels record two instances where Jesus wept tears of sorrow. Once was over a man, Lazarus, his dear friend who had just died. (John 11:35) The other was over a city. As He approached Jerusalem, He looked over her and wept: "O Jerusalem, Jerusalem, you who kill the prophets and stone those sent to you, how often I have longed to gather your children together, as a hen gathers her chicks under her wings" (Matthew 23:37 NIV). This is a picture of Jesus weeping with a grieving love, yet filled with hope. He knew that one day He would make Jerusalem a praise in the earth (Isaiah 62:7) and she would invite Him in saying, "Blessed is he who comes in the name of the Lord" (Matthew 23:39).

Jesus expressed great love for other cities and regions, as well. Samaria was a region that Jesus treated with hope and honor. In Luke 9:51-56, the people of Samaria rejected Him and did not allow for Him to pass through their region because He was on His way to Jerusalem, a city that they despised. The disciples responded with judgment towards Samaria but Jesus rebuked the disciples' response. He understood the enmity between Jews and Samaritans, yet His love and hope for them was greater than the cultural disdain that had characterized their relationships with one another.

A short time later, Jesus used the region of Samaria as an example of tremendous kindness in the parable of the Good Samaritan. This expression of kindness brought healing to the hearts of many Samaritans. It is interesting to note that an entire city in this region was among the earliest to come to faith in Christ after Pentecost (Acts 8:4-8).

JESUS' HOPE AND LOVE FOR THEM WAS GREATER THAN THE CULTURAL DISDAIN.

Jesus did not show contempt for the region of Samaria as His comrades would have. He knew that they would reject Him in the immediate time, but then He saw past their current condition and knew that many in Samaria would come to faith in Him. He had hope in their ultimate destiny and it knew was just around the corner.

Scripture identifies churches by the city in which they were planted. In Revelation 2-3, Jesus speaks to the angels of seven churches, naming them by city. He cared not only for the church, but for the city in which the church existed. He did not separate the two.

Even now, Jesus is at the right hand of His Father interceding for the nations. The nations are His inheritance and the earth is His possession. (Psalm 2:8) Our redeemer Jesus has a certain hope that people from every city and nation on earth will praise Him.

THE MAN OF HOPE

Jesus is the Man of hope. His life on earth is a beautiful illustration of true hope. He had confidence in His Father, deep intimacy in prayer, love for people, hope in the next generation and a redemptive commitment to cities and nations. He is our perfect example as we move forward on our own journey of hope.

chapter ten

HEALING THE SICKNESS
OF HOPELESSNESS

*Man can live about forty days without food, about
three days without water, about eight minutes
without air, but only for one second without hope.*
— Percy Bysshe Shelley

DEBORAH'S DECLARATION OF HOPE

During the first few months Terry and I were on the farm in Zimbabwe, the political unrest in the region continued to escalate. There was a constant sense of danger. The response of fear created feelings of hopelessness in many. When – and how – would it all end? The people on the farm were strong, but it was a new level of challenge for all of us. It was not uncommon for our worship meetings to turn into "worry meetings".

A 15-year old girl named Deborah lived on the farm. This young woman would play the piano each day and sing love songs to Jesus. I often overheard her singing when she thought no one else was listening. In this secret place of worship, she cultivated hope in God. One evening, she came into our prayer meeting and softly declared, "I would rather die in faith than live in fear."

She committed to go out into the nearby village and help the mamas by bringing them the hope she had cultivated inside of herself. Others had become too afraid to venture outside of the farm, but she faced the challenge with a confidence that with God, she would win, no matter what! She was willing to go to others in order to show them the smiling face of Jesus in the midst of their great challenges.

Deborah's example showed me that focusing on Christ in the midst of seemingly-hopeless circumstances allows us to rise above them. It also allows us to bring hope into the lives of those suffering from the soul-sickness of hopelessness.

Hindrances To Hope

Our circumstances can be the number one perpetrator of hopelessness in our souls. But I have found there are also other factors designed by the enemy to breed despair in us instead of allowing us to experience a delighted life.

Accusations of the Enemy

The enemy accuses us in an attempt to bring us into despair. Many do not know how to answer these accusations. They become self-accusers agreeing with the enemy's lies and fabrications about their identities. Like Judas, who suffocated in the shame of betraying Jesus, we can become "accusation centers," destroying our lives and ministries as a result. This is not our destiny. We are called to be "hope centers!"

Accusations produce ripe ground for offense and bitterness to take root in our lives. Often we aren't aware that this bitterness is in us. We become offended at the government, offended at the economy, offended at the church, offended at our own families. We feel entitled and overlooked. We are also vulnerable to the temptation

THE ENEMY ACCUSES US IN AN ATTEMPT TO BRING US INTO DESPAIR.

to accuse God, believing that His care is not sufficient for our situation: "God didn't help and He is not enough".

A life formed by listening to these accusations can solidify into an identity. We no longer live with offense- we become it. If we accept accusation, it can redefine the view we have of ourselves, of God, people, prayer, cities and nations, and the next generation. I had developed an identity formed by accusation until God met me in that Chicago hotel room. As I encountered His true hope, He began setting me free from that toxic identity.

Constant Negativity and Hopelessness

Another hindrance to hope can be a diet of constant negativity and hopelessness. Many years ago Bob Jones told me, "One day there will be twenty-four hour a day bad news being broadcast, spewing negativity and hopelessness versus hope and joy and celebration." At that time, television news consisted of the 6 p.m. and 10 p.m. local news, plus a half hour of national news during the dinner hour. Bob warned that media would be used to infiltrate people with cynicism and doubt, and urged me to be careful where I turned my attention. He said, "Set your eyes on true hope; hope in Him."

I remember his warning every time I turn on the television or the radio. His word became a reality – we are able to constantly fill ourselves with bad news and hopelessness. If we continue, it will lead to doubt addiction.

Doubt Addiction

"Doubt addicts", are people who echo only the problems and pain around them without any hope. Doubt has become a socially-acceptable disease and even considered normal. The truth is, it is a destructive disease. This disease is affecting our children – I had a dream that the enemy wanted to keep the doubt addicts alive to spread doubt and hopelessness to the next generation! I believe the Lord is calling for a decision to move forward into hope, to move from "sorry" to "soaring" so that we will not be overcome by disappointment, desperation and hopelessness.

Wormwood – A Real Spiritual Battle

Revelation speaks of bitter waters that will cover one third of the earth. "The name of the star is Wormwood. A third of the waters turned bitter, and many people died from the waters that had become bitter" (Revelation 8:11 NIV). I once had a dream that helped me understand what might be in these bitter waters. They are waters of despair that can overwhelm our soul when we partner with doubt and unbelief instead of God's goodness. There is a demon of despair that tries to wear down the saints of the Most High (Daniel 7:25). The enemy would like to cause us to drink the waters of despair, causing many to die from the sickness of hopelessness. Others would drink and be as the walking dead, spreading fear, doubt and unbelief as they traveled. But God is bigger than these demons that are trying to have us drink from the waters of despair! Hope is the language of overcomers!

Godly Remedies For Hopelessness

How do we heal this sickness of hopelessness in others and ourselves? How do we bring freedom to doubt addicts?

Magnifying God

God gives each of us a choice: we can magnify the circumstances or we can magnify Him. Everyday we make a choice to listen to the accusation of the enemy or to choose a hopeful view. Many have chosen to pander to their own pain or learn to manage their own brokenness, but the road to health is to encourage each other to journey into the heart of God together.

The hope found in knowing He is near will allow us to face every challenge without questioning His love for us. When circumstances become difficult, we are not to perceive rejection from Him but rather to look for His leading love during the challenges that we face. Hope believes the best about God, even when we do not see or perceive Him in the midst of our day-to-day struggles and trials. We must stop the accusations towards God! It is time to believe that He sees, cares and is more than enough for all of our needs.

HOPE BELIEVES THE BEST ABOUT GOD.

If we let Him, God will turn our anxieties into burning love for Him. He will turn our regrets into redemption. He will turn our doubts and fears about the future into a place of hopeful expectation in Him.

On that farm in Zimbabwe, Deborah purposed to live the truth of Psalm

92:1-2 (NIV): "It is good… to proclaim your love in the morning and your faithfulness at night." This is how we take defeat and turn it into total victory!

Marvelous Comrades

God has given me marvelous comrades who have helped me grow in hope. These are friendships where we don't just identify with each other's misery, but encourage one another to move forward in Christ.

This kind of hope-based friendship can be exemplified by a relationship that I have with a family who lives on the other side of the globe. One of the most challenging struggles I've faced in the last several years has been a battle with ongoing back pain. A few years ago, I was ministering at a conference in Wellington, New Zealand. One of the conference attendees was a highly acclaimed surgeon. Because of the condition of my back, I could not travel back to the U.S. as planned. My friend performed surgery on me as gift. But that's not where his kindness ended.

For the next several months, his family cared for me in their home as I recuperated. During that time, we had nightly prayer gatherings in an upper room of their home. We invited God's presence, hope and love to invade our circumstances and our cities. These times before God brought healing to me and hope to my entire family.

God brings some friends into our lives for the purpose of speaking hope into us. Years ago, Terry and I tried unsuccessfully to have children. When she finally conceived, we were overjoyed...only to have our hopes dashed when she miscarried through the pregnancy. Our friend Brenda sat with us as we grieved, and shared the promise that God had quickened in her – that the Lord would make good on His promise to bless us with children. She painted a picture of hope for us when we could barely see it for ourselves. Her ministry to us restored our hope in the midst of our grief. Today, we rejoice in His gift to us of four children.

The truth is that the Lord does not want us to fight this disease of hopelessness alone. Marvelous comrades help solidify hope within us and help us to fight off the sickness of hopelessness.

Keeping the Testimonies

Another way to guard against the sickness of hopelessness in our own lives is by attending to the testimony God is writing in our lives. "They overcame... by the blood of the Lamb and by the word of their testimony" (Revelation

12:11 NIV). I make it a practice to review my history of hope in God. Our family also spends time at dinner discussing how we experienced God throughout each day. This keeps us focused on what God is doing in our lives instead of being focused on negative circumstances.

HEALTHY IN HOPE

I believe that as we embrace hope in our lives, we will look back at today a year or two from now and ask, "Why did we treat despair as if it had a place in our lives?" Hope is a transforming force that can change not only individual lives, but also nations and generations. Hoping in God and hoping in God through prayer plant a confident expectation for good inside of our souls. By hoping in one another, we will be marvelous comrades that are able to lift people over the misery of the past in order to help them have merry hearts that are filled with hope! By hoping both in the next generation and in cities and nations, miracles will come forth, and His kingdom will advance. Hope transforms everything it touches!

chapter eleven

BECOMING A HOPE CENTER

To them God willed to make known what are the
riches of the glory of this mystery among the Gentiles:
which is Christ in you, the hope of glory.
— Colossians 1:27

WHAT IS A HOPE CENTER?

Once we view all of life through the lenses of a healed and expanded view of God, we will discover we have been supernaturally enabled to walk into each relationship and situation in our lives filled with anticipation to receive good from Him. This expectation is not tied to our circumstances, but flows out of a growing intimacy with the God of all hope. Every aspect of our lives – family, friendships, church, business, recreation, and government – presents an opportunity for us to become a living, breathing "hope center".

A "hope center" is not a building or a physical location. A hope center is YOU, as you choose to cultivate hope and establish the five pillars in the place where you live and function.

People who purpose to become hope centers choose to believe in who God is. This posture releases supernatural power and ability to heal our view of life. Most see the war and the trials in life and lose sight of the God who is triumphant over all. Often we forget to look upward. But this is not the case for people who become hope centers; they keep their focus fixed on God.

THE EARLY CHURCH IS A PROFOUND EXAMPLE OF A HOPE CENTER.

A person or organization that becomes a center of hope can change the atmosphere around them, infusing their sphere of influence with life-giving hope and faith. They are encouragers who deal with disappointments by expressing God's goodness.

HOPE CENTERS BRING REFORMATION

The early church is a profound example of a hope center. Acts 2:44-47 describes a community of believers that had a deep sense of hope in God even in the midst of persecution and tribulation: "All the believers were together and had everything in common. Selling their possessions and goods, they gave to anyone as he had need. Every day they continued to meet together in the temple courts. They broke bread in their homes and ate together with glad and sincere hearts, praising God and enjoying the favor of all the people. And the Lord added to their number daily those who were being saved."

These believers had hope in God and in one another in the midst of the challenges they were facing. The power that went forth from this hope center changed the known world, reforming religion and bringing the good news of the gospel to many cities and nations.

Many of us sense that the present systems of government, economy and even religion are not working. Like the leaders of the early church, we are the appointed reformers of our time. People who are hope centers make the commitment to hope in God in all arenas life, and they bring forth transformation as they hope in Him!

By committing ourselves to a life of hope, we overcome discouragement with encouragement and we overcome fear with faith. We allow the view of God's practical provision for our lives to overshadow our apparent losses. We see that God is supplying and become victorious overcomers, triumphant and full of hope, reforming the world around us.

HABITATIONS OF HOPE –

OUR HOME AS A HOPE CENTER

Hope centers come in many shapes and forms. An individual may function as a one-person hope center. There are also churches, businesses and ministries whose members are filled with hope. These groups can be powerful expressions of hope in their spheres of influence. My own family has taught me much about what it takes to be a hope center.

When Terry and I married, our home was anything but a place of hope. I'd spent my teenage years learning that anger could help me achieve my goals. I would pick fights with my wife just so I could win an argument. I loved winning arguments. My wife has always been very gracious towards me, however, in those days I often put her in a place where her energy had to be channeled towards surviving my negativity instead of thriving in my love. In my unintentional insensitivity, I couldn't see that this contentious atmosphere was wearing on her gentle spirit.

Our time in Zimbabwe quickly leveled the playing field in our marriage. During that challenging season, everything of unimportance stopped. All the busyness of ministry and the frantic hurriedness of life melted away. I had the opportunity to turn from everything else and really discover the unfolding beauty of my wife. We spent a lot of time talking and praying about the years to come if the Lord allowed us to survive our time in the country. It was a vulnerable, tender time. We dreamed of a family and a business, and of creating provision for others and caring for the nations together.

I learned to listen well to my wise, beautiful wife. As I did, I saw how my driven behavior, deeply-rooted anger and hopelessness negatively impacted her. I repented, and purposed to begin to speak and live in a grateful manner.

In the last twenty five years since the Lord first opened my eyes to my sin in this area, hope has transformed our relationship and has become the foundation of our lives together.

Terry and I shared a longing for our family to have a secure foundation in the goodness of God, no matter what the circumstances were. We did not have the language in Zimbabwe to express it, but our prayer was simply that our family would be a true "hope center", a family characterized by hope.

CULTIVATED CELEBRATIONS OF HOPE

Our family has purposed to walk out some practical steps towards becoming a living hope center. There is limitless joy in being a family hope center because together we discover aspects of God that none of us would likely find on our own. My daughter Taylor opens the door to celebration, Bethany opens the door to deep devotion. Amyann shows us how to see others with God's heart. My son, Jedidiah teaches us how to build with wisdom and Terry teaches us how to pray with faith.

Each person's unique walk with God stirs the rest of us to touch the heart of God as he or she has. Our home has become a place centered on loving God and others. It is a place where hope in God has come forth. Here are some practical values that characterize our family hope center.

Hoping in God

Dinner times are sacred for our family as we review what God has done and is doing in our lives. We take turns sharing how we experienced God in hope that day. This helps us to look at life through the lenses of hope in God. We also constantly remind one another of God's promises for us specific to the challenges each one faces.

Hoping in Prayer and in Cities and Nations

Each member of our family brings a different facet of hope needed to form our family as a unique hope center. Terry inspires faith in God and confi-

EACH PERSON'S UNIQUE WALK WITH GOD STIRS THE REST OF US TO TOUCH THE HEART OF GOD AS HE OR SHE HAS.

dence in prayer. When she speaks of His kingdom coming to all nations of the earth, it inspires awe in the rest of us. This awe makes each one of us want to fall on our faces in worship of God.

We make sure to set aside times to pray as a family for our different circumstances and for the people in our lives. We also pray for the nations of the earth to be filled with the glory of God.

Hoping in People and in the Next Generation

My oldest daughter, Amyann, is a champion when it comes to hoping in people. She helps us to constantly remind one another of our identity in God and uniqueness in God. She is consistently mining out the gold in others.

When Amyann was six or seven years old I caught her staring out the back window watching her brother who was chasing a bunny and playing with his imaginary friends. I watched her watching him for several minutes. Then she turned to me with a smile and said, "My, my, Dad, you have such a special son." She regularly takes time to appreciate the beauty in others.

To be a true hope center is to constantly affirm one another and recognize the treasure in each one. As a family hope center, we practice affirming one another. We make it a lifestyle to believe in others, opening our home to them and loving them.

Wisdom

My son, Jedidiah, is becoming a noble king, full of graciousness and gentleness. He has a maturity and wisdom that is beyond his years. He is hungry for the wisdom of God. When Jed was eleven years old, I took him with me to clean theaters one night. I gave him a mop and told him to go at it! After a few minutes, I returned to check on Jed and found him leaning on his mop, observing the employees.

Naturally, I told him to get going! But he began to share with me divine insight for the business. He laid out a plan for the placement of personnel. By observing their interactions with one another, he discerned which employees would work best together, and how to motivate each one. He is an anointed observer, like Solomon in I Kings 10, where the Queen of Sheba came to observe his wisdom and it was his practical wisdom that astounded her:

> *When the queen of Sheba perceived all the wisdom of*
> *Solomon, the house that he had built, the food of his table,*

the seating of his servants, the attendance of his waiters and their attire, his cupbearers, and his stairway by which he went up to the house of the LORD, there was no more spirit in her. (I Kings 10: 4-5 NASB)

Jed has this ability to see the practical wisdom of the Lord applied to everyday life. He is a king in the making!

WE LAUGH AT THE ENEMY'S LIES AND PLANS AGAINST OUR LIFE.

We seek after the wisdom of heaven as a family by spending a part of our evenings sitting together discussing the Word of God. We are hungry to discover His truths together and apply them to our everyday lives.

Joy and Laughter

My daughter Taylor, bring joys to our family hope center. We always have fun when we are around her.

One day several years ago, Taylor came home from school discouraged because a classmate had been teasing her.

She told our family what she was going through at school and provided herself with a solution; the next thing we knew, she was on the ground, having a belly laugh! Taylor has taught us all how to laugh at our problems.

We practice joy and celebration as a lifestyle even when circumstances are difficult and challenging. We laugh at the enemy's lies and plans against our life. Hope centers must be filled with this kind of joy and laughter.

Devotion

Bethany, our youngest child, has a deep, deep devotion to God and to people. She is our delight and faithfully serves the dreams and cares of our hearts. When I had surgery in New Zealand a few years ago, Bethany flew out to care for me. For weeks while I was recovering, she waited on me, hand and foot, instinctive about my needs without me having to ask. This nine-year-old little girl showed me what it is to be truly devoted to one another.

We take time to give devotion and adoration to the Lord together as a family. One way we've done this is by going through the letters of the alphabet, naming the attributes of God. We praise Him: "God, you are Awesome, Beautiful, Compassionate, Delightful."

Love without Offense

In a true hope center, love rules. In our family, we choose to replace offense towards one another with love. Like any family, we have given each other plenty of opportunities for offense. But by the grace of God, we have purposed to have hope in the love of the others. We are vigilant, not allowing bitterness and offense to pollute our love.

I can remember Terry and I were in an argument and she broke out in a laugh that shattered the intensity. "Why even go there?" she giggled. And that was that. It doesn't always happen that way for us, but as a hope center we fight for love above all else.

Preparation for Life

Preparation for life is possible in a hope center. My children do not avoid the future. Instead, they look to it with hopeful eyes. Success is accepted, as each individual is believed in and celebrated. We have become each other's cheerleaders and promise keepers.

Supernatural Activity

Hope centers are also catalysts for the supernatural. My children come to me regularly in order to share the dreams and pictures the Lord has given them about what God is doing in the earth. They have an uncompromising hope for cities and nations, the next generation, and people. They recognize the miracles of God happening around them.

Reformation

Hope centers breed reformers. My children have impacted their friends and schools with hope, and have even touched cities and nations with their influence. My wife is changing nations through hopeful prayer and action. This is the result of true hope in God: reformation.

OTHER TYPES OF HOPE CENTERS

Businesses

Businesses can be another form of a true hope center. God gives ingenuity and creativity to business hope centers built on His promises. Employees at hope center businesses are encouraged to seek God's creative solutions for customers. Bosses at hope center businesses express care and confidence in their employees. This hope spills into the community.

We have committed to make our business a hope center for the marketplace of Kansas City. The Hartley Group is comprised of five businesses and our ministry Deeper Waters. We live out the five pillars of hope in practical ways throughout the day. As a kingdom company, we exercise our hope in God by meeting every morning for adoration prayer. We magnify and extol the Lord for His attributes that we see in the business and in one another. We develop our hope in people as we encourage one another and call forth the gifting and the destiny bestowed upon each one by the Father. We treat our subcontractors and tenants in the same manner, focusing upon who they are in God rather than who they are not. We exercise our hope in the next generation by walking out our value of mentoring youth and young adults in the business. We have many interns who come to learn daily life skills and how to cultivate communion with God all throughout the day!

We exercise our hope in prayer by being committed to building on our knees! We bring our perceived challenges in our specific areas in the business, and we lay them at the feet of Jesus, choosing to see those challenges as opportunities for miracles and encounter with Him. We exercise our hope in cities and nations by pouring resources into nations like Zimbabwe, where we are believing for transformation through hope in God!

Schools

Schools can also be hope centers. My Dad was a hope reformer for the school he oversaw. He played classical music in the hallways and took every opportunity he could to celebrate individual students. He also helped to create an innovative program using the playground area of the school grounds to create colorful maps, math facts, and sight words. This playground-learning environment was such a success that PM Magazine, a nationally broadcast news program, profiled his efforts. Dad was dedicated to making the urban school a haven of hope for children as he incorporated fun in learning.

WE EXERCISE OUR HOPE IN PRAYER BY BUILDING ON OUR KNEES.

The Daniel Academy is another example of a school hope center. The Daniel Academy is a Kindergarten through 12th grade school based in Kansas City designed to develop present day "Daniels" like Daniel of the Bible. The Daniel Academy is a hope center for young people, both training them to be influencers and instilling in them the core values of prayer and living a life consecrated to God. The school is developing young people who are well educated and trained in both academics and spiritual understanding, cultivating pure hearts, endowed with discernment, and having the ability to serve in the courts of the present day kings (Daniel 1:4).

Churches

Bethel Church in Redding, CA is an example of a church that is a Hope Center for the nations. Pastors Bill and Beni Johnson and their team are pioneering a new type of church that carries a culture of life, hope and joy. Miracles of healing, provision and power have come forth from this center of renewal as they have focused on the nature of God and lived from the core value that He is always good!

There is no 1-2-3 formula to make your family, business, school or church a hope center. It begins as you commit to boldly live out the hope God has placed within you.

The Invitation For You

God is inviting each one of us to be a living, breathing hope center. As we accept this invitation, transformation happens. As we begin to place God at the center of our lives and adopt a lifestyle of hope, we become influencers of every arena of life. For all of us there is an opportunity to become habitations of His glory and His hope, spreading hope to all those we encounter.

chapter twelve
THE FORCE OF HOPE

Those who hope in the Lord will renew their strength.
They will soar on wings like eagles; they will run
and not grow weary, they will walk and not be faint.
— Isaiah 40:31 NIV

A FINAL WORD FROM AMYANN

My father asked me to add some final thoughts about the hope journey. I pray the chapters and stories you have read thus far have been like a fire of hopefulness setting your heart ablaze and that you have been led into an encounter with our God, the God of hope.

As his daughter, I have had the privilege of watching my dad walk out the hope journey that the Lord has directed him to walk. He has "walked the talk" by pursing hope in God for himself and for the sake of others, including each one of us in his family.

I have observed how hope in God has transformed my dad from a broken man, driven by fear and a need to succeed, to a man who is a patriarch of hope, believing and bringing out the best in others and calling forth the beautiful possibilities of life.

One of the most profound ways that Dad discovered true hope in God was through his own father, my grandfather who was a man of great hope and love. My grandfather's life of hope was passed on to my father who, in turn, gave me a path of hope on which to walk. This hope legacy, this hope journey, is a gift of true hope in God that is not only my inheritance from my father and grandfather, but offered as an inheritance to you as well from our heavenly Father who has given us every good gift under heaven.

The Spiral Notebooks Of Hope

My grandfather pioneered his walk of hope in everyday life through everyday circumstances. My dad has been greatly influenced by his father's journey of hope in God.

Dad has struggled with ongoing back problems for many years. (The Lord is doing a healing work in his body and our family and friends are believing God for full restoration of his body.) Dad had his first back surgery shortly after graduating from college. My grandparents invited him back into their home to care for him after he was released from the hospital. He accepted their offer. This was to be the first time he would be back under their roof since he left home as a young teenager.

During his childhood, his family's home was often a place of turmoil. Because of my grandmother's own back injury, she was bedridden for years and I understand the atmosphere around the home was quite challenging for everyone.

However, during this stay he found the condition of the home quite different. His parents' home was now filled with hope and joy! He began to wonder how this beautiful transition had taken place, and what could have been the catalyst for this great change in the atmosphere? His questions were answered in a surprising way when he discovered a beautiful secret to His dad's journey of hoping in God.

One day as he was lying in the spare bedroom resting, he reached underneath the bed looking for some reading materials. It was dusty and dirty under the bed since no one had been in this room for years. He pulled out an old cardboard box filled with spiral notebooks. As he began to read, he realized he had discovered his father's journals. The pages were filled with almost-daily entries of hopeful prayers to God.

THE NEXT SECTION OF THE HOPEFUL PRAYER READ, "BUT THEN I KNOW BOBBY WILL PIN HIS PROBLEMS TO THE MAT."

Inside each of the journals, my grandfather had created three columns. The first column was labeled "challenges", the second column, "prayers", and the third was titled "God's answers". Dad read about the way his father lifted up his concerns to the Lord. For instance, my grandfather prayed, "Dear Lord, let Anne walk again. Let her know she is the princess I married. Let her feel the warmth of Your love." He interceded for my grandmother, who had been experiencing debilitating back problems.

Dad continued to read on to the "hope answer" column. There was a thankful and victorious account of my grandmother's restored health. "Thank you, thank you Lord!" He wrote, "Anne is walking again!" The Lord had miraculously healed my grandmother after seven years of being bedridden! She had begun to walk and come alive again, blooming in God's goodness and my grandfather's love for her. Dad thought about how his father's prayers for her were answered. My grandmother and grandfather were like a prince and a princess until the day my grandfather died. My grandfather always had such hope for her and in her!

My dad discovered his father's prayers for him in those journals as well. Dad's eyes blurred with tears as he read the scrawled handwriting: "Bobby is not doing well. I'm afraid he is going to make some poor decisions." The next section, the hopeful prayer, read, "But then I know Bobby will pin his problems to the mat and be a great man. He will touch so many lives."

The way my grandfather hoped in God for his circumstances that seemed so dark at the time is amazing. As Dad lay on the guestroom bed reading those journals, the Lord showed him what the daily battle for hope looked like. It was a choice to hope in God's goodness and abilities no matter what is thrown his way or no matter what is difficult in life. God is more than enough for every challenge!

From that experience, I believe my Dad realized that if he allowed himself to enter into despair, he would run from the challenges of the day. But if he chose to hope each day as my grandfather did, then he could move forward and attack life, undaunted by the obstacles. Dad has made a decision in his life, and we have made this choice as a family: when perceived challenges come, we will continue to fight with a hope not grounded in positive circumstances, but in an eternal decision to believe that no matter what happens, with God, we will always win!

THE "HOPE JOURNEY"

The Lord is inviting the body of Christ worldwide on a journey of hope. My grandfather left an inheritance of hope for my father through the spiral notebooks and the way that he lived his life as an example in hope. My father has also left me an inheritance of hope in God.

A journey towards hope in God is a holy process into the presence and person of Jesus, where we are empowered to walk as hope reformers and hope bringers that carry the force of hope throughout all of life, transforming cities and nations for His glory. The Lord has always given us a way of wisdom to enter into His presence, as He did with Moses, David and Solomon.

My father has modeled what it looks like to not only begin a journey of hope, but to continue on that journey in order to build hope into others, in every area of life. This journey begins in prayer, continues step by step with the Lord through daily life, and draws near to Him in trust through seeking His counsel for every challenge in order to establish the five hope pillars. The following are the steps of the hope journey that the Lord has invited him and all of us to follow.

Step 1: Begin The Journey In The Hope Room

This hope journey begins in the Hope Room. The Hope Room is our secret place with God where we love Him first, and develop an attitude of the heart where God's nature is declared in all life situations. In the Hope Room, He is magnified above the circumstances! As David wrote, "Glorify the Lord with me, let us magnify the Lord together" (Psalm 34:3 NIV). It is in the Hope Room that the knowledge of God is unlocked in new ways. Here we are filled with God's presence and begin to see all of life from God's heavenly perspective.

In the Hope Room, we become equipped to understand who God is in us, as we proclaim His nature in one another and ourselves. In the Hope Room, we also rewrite our histories through the lens of Hope in God. In order for us to be able to build a life in hope, and hear clearly from the Lord, we must remove the old offenses and stumbling blocks from our past. We must learn to see our past through the lens of hope in order to discover the ways that God was there building our future. He was near even when we did not perceive Him or believe in His goodness. Thus, our past becomes redefined according to a redemptive view. In the Hope Room we also remember and give thanks for all the miracles and mighty deeds that the Lord has done for us. Our eyes are lifted as we cultivate a heart of thankfulness! Beginning in the place of prayer will set our course for the next step of the journey.

Step 2: The Through Street –
Following Jesus Into Each Day

The next step is simply to live out what has been settled inside of us during our time in the hope rooms. We learn to commune and partner with God throughout the day in every season. In our spiritual lives, we can so often define our spiritual walk to the time we spend at church, in prayer or reading the Bible. These times are fundamental; however, the Lord wants to expand our perspective to see Him in every room of our house, our workplace and in every area of our lives. He does not want to be confined to a Sunday, but wants us to commune with Him throughout everyday. He wants to be invited into business, education, politics, family and our cities and nations. Step 2 of our journey in hope is discovering for ourselves that He is the God of all of life.

Step 3: The Counsel Table
Of The Lord Where
We Stop To Listen To Him

The next step of the journey is where we come to the Counsel Table of the Lord and commune with Him on a deeper level. The Counsel Table Of The Lord is a way of describing the process where we can come before Him in prayer to learn his strategies for the challenges we face on the journey. At the Counsel Table Of The

WE MUST LEARN TO SEE OUR PAST THROUGH THE EYES OF HOPE.

Lord, we learn to listen to His creative solutions for the problems we encounter.

The Lord has invited us into a partnership, a place of authority where He extends the invitation for us to build with Him through hope. At the Counsel Table of the Lord, He lays out the blueprints, and gives us clever ideas and witty inventions to bring hopeful solutions to our lives.

Step 4: Establishing The Hope Pillars
And Building With Him In All Of Life

As we learn to trust Him in prayer and in our daily life, we understand that hope is at the core of our ministry. We will be people who establish pillars of hope – in God, in people, in the next generation, in prayer and in cities and nations!

Choosing To Be A Hope Bringer

Hope orients us toward God. The world tries to convince us that riches and comfort are the goal of our lives, but in the end, these things leave us with an empty existence and hollow defeat. Our hearts were designed to be filled with the fullness of God and we are to experience the richness of being champions of hope in Him. No lesser reality will do!

Living a life of hope is a counter-cultural way to live and it is the way of Jesus. This "narrow road" journey will help you discover more of God Himself than you can contain. You will taste of an incredible life of celebrating friendship with Him. Your hope will be contagious. This hope that has the power to transform everything it touches!

OUR INHERITANCE IN HOPE

My grandfather and father have passed on an inheritance of hope that I am tapping into as I live each day. But this inheritance isn't limited to the Hartley family. Hope is an inheritance that belongs to you if you are a child of God. This inheritance of hope is His gift of love to you.

Express that hope in word and deed. And proclaim that hope in prayer. Here are some proclamations of hope that you can use to equip you for the journey of hope to which He has called you:

Proclamations of Hope:

As we choose to hope in You, we will be focused on a favorable future.

As we choose to hope in You, we will go from having despair in trials to persevering in them!

As we choose to hope in You, we will go from defeat to victory in You!

As we choose to hope in You, we will not live in mediocrity but will be confident of our great significance. We will not be apathetic about life, but appreciate every moment.

As we choose to hope in You, we will not produce skepticism and doubt, but build faith with expectation for good.

As we choose to hope in You, we will move from remorse about our sin to true repentance.

As we choose to hope in You, we will move from being victims of demonic harassment to those who are aware of the angelic assistance God provides for us.

As we choose to hope in You, we will turn sadness and anger to joy and laughter.

As we choose to hope in You, we will go from enslavement to freedom. We will no longer be displeased with ourselves, but satisfied in who we are.

As we choose to hope in You, we will not strive for existence, be inactive or merely busy, we will be hard working and productive.

As we choose to hope in You, we will become life givers and problem-solvers.

As we choose to hope in You, we won't stop with just reading about history, we will make history!

As we choose to hope in You, we will be characterized by generosity. Gratitude, strength, joy and fulfillment characterize those whose hope is in God alone!

As we choose to hope in You, God's kingdom is advanced in our world, and You allow us to go where You go and do what You do as we travel together into the future.

As we choose to hope in You, we will go from being skeptical of God's existence and character to being secure in His promises.

As we choose to hope in You, we will go from an unstable foundation, to a firm foundation of faith.

As we choose to hope in You, we will no longer distrust authority but trust and honor those in authority over us.

As we choose to hope in You, we won't expect a "hand out" but we will offer others a "hand up".

As we choose to hope in You, we won't be draining on others, but we will be life giving to them. We will not tear others down, but we will build them up.

As we choose to hope in You, instead of being the problem, we will solve the problem!

As we choose to hope in You, we will go from being a negative influence to a positive influence.

As we choose to hope in You, we will go from cursing others to blessing others. We will stop blaming others for errors and take responsibility for our own mistakes.

As we choose to hope in You, we will go from not trusting God or people to trusting Him and believing in others.

As we choose to hope in You, we will go from illness to divine health.

As we choose to hope in You, we will move from financial dependency and poverty, to financial sufficiency and contentment.

As we choose to hope in You, we will go from bitterness to gratitude.

As we choose to hope in You, we will go from hopeless delusions to sound reasoning.

As we choose to hope in You, we will move from frustrated and empty, to being fulfilled.

As we choose to hope in You, we will go from having unbalanced priorities to being balanced and wise in our priorities.

As we choose to hope in You, we will stop elevating the trivial and instead we will elevate what is truly important.

As we choose to hope in You, we will not just survive in a holding pattern, but we will advance the Kingdom of God!

As we choose to hope in You, we will go from a temporal focus to an eternal perspective.

As we choose to hope in You, we will no longer see curveballs in life as burdensome, but humorous!

As we choose to hope in You, we will go from seeing darkness to seeing light, from seeing nothing good to seeing powerful potential.

As we choose to hope in You, we will not return to our past with regret or despair but look to the future with anticipation.

As we choose to hope in You, we will no longer have blocked creativity but we will become dreamers in You!

As we choose hope in You, we will go from good to great. We will move from glory to glory in this wondrous journey of hope!

Further Interest

Chapter Five

Terry's effort in Zimbabwe is called Project: Generation Hope. More information about the project can be found at http://www.projectgenerationhope.org.

Chapter Eight

To learn more about this story, please See George Otis, Jr.'s DVD, "Let the Sea Resound" about the transformation of Fiji at http://www.sentinelgroup.org.

Chapter Eleven

For more information about The Daniel Academy visit http://www.thedanielacademy.com.

Chapter Twelve

To learn about resources to help you walk out each step of the Hope Journey, visit www.bobhartley.org.

Hope Building Blocks

Hope Kit- $85

This Hope Kit includes the best Hope feedings to launch you into your journey of hope! This kit includes: The Hope DVD Series, New Adoration Prayer Book, The Call to the Wall Book, and Four Prayer CD's (Face of God as Redeemer, Supplier, Builder and the Wise God).

Adoration Prayer Booklet
$15.00 (2 for $25, 3 for $30)

The Adoration Prayer Booklet is an advanced tool that helps you to develop your own love language with the King of Kings, guiding you into deep adoration and intimacy with our beautiful God through devotional prayer. This book is an exploration of the attributes and character of our Great God, arranged by the letters of the alphabet, with scriptural references and sections for journaling and adding in your own examples and heartfelt language. Great for children and families too!

Hope Prayer CD's- Each $10.00

This Hope prayer CD series, features Bob Hartley modeling adoration with the four Forgotten Faces of God to be discovered in 2009-2011. Each CD models one of these faces, the Redeemer God, the Supplier God, the Builder God and the Wise God. We encourage you to buy the set of four for a great discount, and build your love language with the Lord, unlocking these faces of God in your business, family and everyday life.

Heart of Adoration CD- $15

For years, Bob Hartley has drawn people into greater intimacy with Jesus through his prayers of Adoration. Now, in the 'Prayers of Adoration' series, these prayers are captured for you, making it easy to add a fresh spark of intimacy to your own personal prayer life. 'Heart of Adoration' focuses on 'Why We Adore God'. These prayers, coupled with instrumental music, provide an inspiring tool that will carry you into the heart of a passionate pursuing God.

Jesus Man of Hope Prayer CD- $10

This CD in the Hope prayer CD series, features Bob Hartley adoring Jesus the Man of Hope, and how He hoped in His Father, how He hoped in People and called out the greatness in them, how He hoped in the next generation, and how He hoped in Cities and Nations. This is a powerful tool of devotion that will strengthen your love language with God and bring you into encounter with Jesus the man of hope.

52 Weeks of Hope- $20 per month

Each week, Bob Hartley and the Deeper Waters team have recorded special "fireside chats" where Bob and others share the most important keys for living an abundant life in God with a living hope for today! Receive one-on-one mentoring from Bob and the Deeper Waters team. This weekly 10 minute video clip is sent directly to your email, and includes practical building blocks to apply to your week, as you embark on this journey of hope! Sign up at 52weeksofhope.com

Centcom Broadcast every Tuesday night- **FREE

Don't miss our weekly "Hope Broadcast" on Centcom.tv that gives great practical building blocks and insight into the heart of God for the present hour in the Body of Christ. Broadcast every Tuesday night at 7pm, and archived for the remainder of the week, is a fresh teaching on how to live as a Hope Reformer and impact your family, business, city and nation with the life-changing force of Hope in God!

All tools available on our website

www.bobhartley.org